Tell them today what they will remember tomorrow and forever

DB Smith

I would like to thank my wife and children for the time, support, and love they gave me to share my insights and perspective on fatherhood. Without their contributions, this book would be full of empty pages.

For more information, please visit:
www.workingclassdad.com

TABLE OF CONTENTS

Intro

I am a father of five children. That statement, as it is written, takes my mind back in time. Most teenagers or young adults don't actually consider the specific details involved with being a parent. At least I didn't. I don't think I ever once considered what life would be like as a father. I never contemplated what my dad was experiencing or the challenges that could be faced when attempting to care and provide for other human beings. But I assure you, the responsibilities are very well realized now. And I have found it to be the most challenging and rewarding endeavor one can ever take on. To attempt to meet children's individual needs takes a monumental amount of creativity and intentional energy. Interactions and conversations have ranged from diaper changes to dating to driving, and at times, all in the same day. All three examples can present their own individually complex set of challenges. My experience as a father is not incomparable in the sense of what every day is like in the life of any dad who is trying to find his way in this role. I will confess, I am not an expert on parenting or clinical psychology. But I believe my qualifications to write this book will be revealed as I share stories and the discovery of a secret recipe that has made me regret that I didn't start earlier. I will give you the secret recipe near the end of the book, but don't turn there now, because it will be impossible to cook without the list of ingredients along the way. The sole purpose of this book is to help you find your own version of the recipe for becoming a better father and to encourage you to take advantage of the time you have with your children as you balance your work and home life.

My first daughter was born when I was twenty years old. What I remember most about the experience was the unparalleled and unequivocal joy I felt when she first came into this great big world. The only fair explanation is to say life kicked in the door and flooded it with absolute joy. But within mere seconds I realized that I hadn't heard her first cry because she wasn't breathing. I immediately experienced panic as the next very raw emotion. I had never been a part of childbirth, my only idea of what to expect in the delivery room was from a television scene. Baby is born, baby cries; and this wasn't the case. Fear gripped me as my entire world dangled by a thread. I momentarily thought about the unknowns. I couldn't imagine losing her. I watched the frantic nurses move back and forth and then I turned my attention to the doctor again as he held her upside down and smacked her bottom which prompted a cry that is forever embedded in the auditory code of my being. Hearing that cry for the first time, especially after a roller coaster of emotions that seemed to pass in slow motion, was quite the entry and initiation to fatherhood. I have since shared in the honor, privilege, and experience of the delivery room four more times all while supporting their wonderful mother. Today, all of our children are alive and healthy, and that is all we ever hoped for.

So, what exactly does it mean to be a father? What is the overall need when it comes to raising a child correctly or can you even do it? Are you equipped? Do you have a plan? Do you just wing it? So many questions, so few guiding lights. When I look back over the past twenty years of being a father, there are things I have done right and of course, many things I have done wrong. I am grateful for having children that are patient with me as I try to get this right as well. To speak to those errors, I have most often harmed my intentions and efforts by incorrectly prioritizing my work over my family. It is nearly impossible to make yourself aware of the problem. But it's effortlessly conceivable that we feel guilty about working too much in the wake of missing out on anything important. And that is exactly how the bad habit starts. You miss one event or forget something special and before you know what's hit you, you've entered a full-blown cycle of confusion.

We love our family, it's just that the opposing force to that guilt is the natural need and desire to provide for our family. So, there you are, trying to make sense of your commitments and how to prioritize them without losing your job or losing your children. If we didn't live in a world structured around commerce and business, we wouldn't necessarily feel guilty about staying out all night hunting for food or finding ways to provide shelter for our families. On the other hand, thankfully today, that isn't a common problem we have. Which tells me we are allotted and allowed the privilege to plan and prioritize our life. So, we are going to work on ways to learn what's important and what's not. Your job is very important as it is the means by which you provide for your home. I am going to discuss topics that may feel like I am against it, but please don't confuse it with just getting your priorities in order. As fathers in the workforce, we have crucial deadlines to meet, projects to forever work on, and goals to be passionately realized. And most of those are just at home.

Is it possible to get work and fatherhood in proper balance? You control the final answer to that. The probability is increased only if you become intentional and work at it with the same passion to do any other task set before you. Maybe the tools look a little different, but the work on both sides of your day involve the same person; you. What I plan to uncover in this book are the insights and applications to parenting that maybe you haven't considered but could be easily introduced. When I consider the more experienced father I am today, compared to the one I was in the beginning, my only regret is that I didn't practice the things I do with my children now. If only I would've had someone share this with me earlier! And I can't imagine what my life would be like now without the lessons I have learned and the connections I have built with my children and the level of confidence, belief, and happiness I have seen develop mightily within them. So many opportunities missed, but now I have the solution and I don't have to live with the regrets any longer because I have experienced the success. And I can build on that for the future. Hope is not lost.

Why is it that when we introduce ourselves in a room full of people, as men, we typically focus on this question first - "what do you do for a living?" Typically, our go-to is to talk about our work and maybe even our projects or responsibilities in more detail. Following work, we may even entertain discussing our sports team, hobbies, or favorite foods. We are men, and that type of conversation is perfectly ok. Welcome to the animal kingdom. But why don't we spend much time talking about our families? Talking about family is typically considered to be more private for most individuals. But, over the years, I have experienced much more meaningful and deeper conversations and connections with people if they know that I am a platform for that type of talk. Which again proves to me, that finding resolution or understanding for those specific areas are the perplexities of life that truly interest us the most, but we are just thoroughly conditioned to not talk about it. But if we never talk about those relationships, how can we properly fix anything. And that is what men naturally do when they need to work on something new, they talk about it or recruit some help to do it. And as men, we have a desire to fix everything. Even if it's not broken, sometimes we try to fix it until it is.

Failure in the workplace or in business in general is easier to overcome than failure in a valued relationship. Heartbreak and frustration are brutal realities, and broken communication because of simple errors can be the usual culprit. And it doesn't just happen by surprise or overnight. It really happens in quite a sneaky way. It is the culmination of tiny interactions that lead to become the true hidden iceberg in the water. Your mighty ship will turn upwards to the sky when it hits. Shipwrecked and going down is never fun, as history has shown. If you feel that void in your relationship now, don't worry, those bonds of trust and respect can be rekindled.

Recently, I had a colleague from our senior management team visiting our office to discuss potential business, projects, and forecasts that didn't leave much room for the personal conversations and aspects of who we are individually. Nothing out of the norm, this is standard behavior and practices we are accustomed to in business. It is the reason businesses stay in business. But this colleague stayed after the meeting we were both in, and like a magnet, we were drawn together to discuss our families. We had spoken in the past about personal things involving fatherhood, and he knew I was an open book to talk and discuss the challenges and fringe thoughts on parenting. And I valued his insights and thoughts as well. You don't easily forget the people you connect with who authentically value what you share and can genuinely offer their own fresh perspective. It's called compassion. He was experiencing heavy confusion and frustration because of a 16-year-old girl who was living in his home, who called him dad. He was completely desperate for a solution. What I shared with him helped me to see that I no longer needed to keep my secret for healthy, open communication. The impact inspired me as one of the initial reasons I wanted to pursue this undertaking of writing a book that could bridge the gap between any father and any child.

Shortly after that talk, I again shared my secret with a young lady on the plane I met on my way back to Detroit. She cried her eyes out. She revealed the exact pain in her relationship with her father and that she just wished that her dad would make time for her and stop spending all his time at work. It served as another reminder to me that this is a real problem. A man can get tied into his work or his own mind and totally miss the complete relevance of his existence. Some cultures globally and some ways of thinking even in the good old US of A, revolve around the idea that our sole purpose in life is to work. In my gut, I cannot get behind this idea. Provision is the essential driving force in the mind of a man when it comes to the thoughts and considerations of his family. However, you can take it too far. Balance becomes a distant memory and those habits you form as you overdo it become normalized to the point that you disconnect from the people you love. Eventually becoming extremely self-centered and isolated. All while the ones you love are longing for you but feel trapped because they feel hopeless and that the conversation would not be welcome or even on your radar as important.

Foundationally, all relationships are built on four pillars. They are trust, respect, forgiveness, and commitment. All of which are the platform of love. It is nearly impossible to be in a thriving relationship with one of these in a damaged state. Within our day to day operations, we operate within the boundaries of trust and respect with the ones we love. When we fail or do something to break trust or respect, we need forgiveness to get back to good. And without commitment, one can completely lose the value and energy to continue to pursue the relationship. It is quite silly to think that if I just do something wrong as a father, I can just throw out a simple "I'm sorry" and all my problems go away. But I've got bad news for you. That is not how it works. Some fathers may not have ever considered that forgiveness is something that needs to be discussed or even requested with your children. But I assure you that it is. In all relationships, there are multitudes of opportunities to make mistakes, and in them we should always seek to make things right first. As a father, you can't wait. It is your duty and responsibility. We will look at each one of the pillars in depth in the chapters to come and will focus on ways to apply lasting methods and restore broken ties. That doesn't mean this will be easy, but nonetheless highly necessary. Just don't give up!

Ideally, I want to setup a strong base model or reference for you as you plan out a strategy to form strong relationships with the ones you love so dearly. There are going to be several topics that we need to cover before we get to the meat and potatoes. First, we will look more deeply into the pillars of every good relationship, how to effectively communicate, and how to create an atmosphere for growth in any setting. Following this, we will break down a father's true role and the main functions demonstrated within this patriarchal responsibility. Wrapping it up, we will cover the implementation of building a solid and lasting connection that will pass down through the ages for your generations to come. I want you to stay business minded in this, as we will be comparing our work experiences and finding glaring similarities to the way we conduct ourselves inside the home. But know this, by the end, we will move away from the office and focus on the absolute true topics that matter. I hope you enjoy this, as I begin to write the subject matter that is written on my heart. My desire is that this manual will afford you the strength and effort to create stronger bonds in your relationships and that you find your own unique voice and recipe.

A last word of encouragement before we start. I would highly recommend reading this book with another father to discuss what you've read to make sense of it and help you find ways to apply the ideas into your life. I know for sure that I wouldn't be the father I am today if I didn't have friends and family that are fathers that gave me insights when I needed them. Far too many to count at this point. But a network of fathers is better than a network in business. Don't forget that. That business network is important in regard to your career, but it will fade long before the life you lead at home. We must realize there is real strength in sharing with each other as men and putting forth real effort to communicate and grow the relationships we value.

Chapter 1 | Communication

Grunting, growling and groaning are not great forms of communication when it comes to parenting. But through our expressionless face and quiet demeanor, we can so easily walk back into the cave as a father. I intend to help you stay out of the cave. There are moments that each of those behaviors feel completely natural. Work through them in both your family life and in your place of business. At the end of this book I plan to unveil to you a way to solidify the bonds with your children through a very simple form of communication. But the requirement for successfully applying the practice requires you to consider my advised methodology and approach for your desired results. If you will commit to the basic ideals and principles I lay out, it will fully equip you to be a high performing father. Not a perfect father, but one who believes in himself and the effort he puts forth.

When any individual sets out to learn something new, they dedicate time and energy to allow for improvement. Just because you are a father, it doesn't mean you are not constantly trying to find ways to improve. So often, I think we view parenting as a state of default rather than something we should be constantly striving to improve with. As you may know, when you purchase a home with a mortgage attached, they don't forget about that debt the moment you have a housewarming party. No, exact opposite, they want to extend a long relationship to you and send you letters every month to remind you how much they love you... Maybe not, but you get the picture. Just because you became a father, doesn't mean you just exist as one now. It takes hard work and you must be intentional and doing everything you can to improve.

Be proactive

How do you approach your children today? I don't care what age they are; but what do you do? How do you go about it? Do you call them? Do you set apart time for them? Do you pursue building a relationship with them or do you just run damage control? From my past experiences, the best companies I have worked for seem to be very intentional about how they manage employee communications and feedback. The terminology for the effort utilized is very basic. Proactive or reactive. In communication, this can be detrimental to any situation in the workplace, whether its safety related or just in daily interactions. For example, a company that allows its employees freedom to make observations that may prevent harm or find potential for a dangerous situation, it is proactive. A company that is reactive allows an injury, incident, or accident to happen by only noticing the risk or event when it happens, then addressing it. One of my past responsibilities in a management role was to go out and seek out these types of potential risks and document my findings daily. It was a shared responsibility between the management team. Sometimes, it may have been as simple as material or a product being stacked in such a way that it could be damaged. For others, it may have been much more serious. So serious, that a life may even be at risk. It may be more than material being damaged if someone didn't follow certain procedures or guidelines for how to stack certain product. The material could potentially fall off the top of the stack and land on someone if it wasn't done correctly. The reason the material would be stacked incorrectly was because of a very well-known culprit. In a high production volume plant, it was important to get your job done quickly, but some people would tend to rush rather than pay attention and do a good job, even if it took a little more time. When people rush through anything, it becomes exponentially more likely that they will make a mistake. Our job was to find those mistakes and hopefully prevent potential injuries and accidents. And although at times, it may have felt like redundant work, when you were able to find something that could have potentially saved someone's life, you quickly realized the value of performing those tasks. And communicating those internally within the company helped others to realize the value as well. If they were applicable catches that could save lives, we would study the situation and find ways to eliminate the opportunities to repeat them. It was also our responsibility to discuss and challenge our employees to find these as well. If we had an accident or injury, we would also stop all production and bring all employees to the site and discuss what happened openly and how we could prevent these types of things.

For parenting, I would highly suggest the method I am promoting in this book, which is proactive. You won't eliminate surprise, but you have a much better shot if your communicating clearly and using real life examples to help your child make the best of their life. There will be times when those observations you are making will feel quite redundant and you may not fully understand why you are doing it. But, when the time comes and you help them to avoid something in their life that could potentially harm them, it will all make sense. I am not telling you to be a new age "helicopter parent", which means you constantly hover over your child in a way that doesn't allow them to grow and have their own life experience. If anything, I am telling you to find the happy medium where you find correction and guidance at the heart. A child should be able to make mistakes, no matter the age. Your child can make mistakes just like you still do, even at your age.

Boundaries

Proper boundaries must be set for any relationship. Crossing over other people's boundaries can have dire consequences. Some people may never let you know you crossed the line; they just simply disappear. Others may react violently. Boundaries we define as human beings are simply our internal user's manual for what we are willing to accept. Be cautioned, there may be different manuals designed for different people. We may be more understanding with people we know have our best interest at hand, but with a stranger, become highly offended by the simplest interaction. Boundaries are tied to personal conviction shaped by experience and understanding of the world around us. The complexity is too vast to really describe in great length, but important to understand. Plenty of outstanding works of literature dedicated to just that topic are available online or at any bookstore. In your children, it may seem that this changes from minute to minute depending on the age. But I assure you I have a proven way for you to navigate the landmines buried along the way or at least not take on any life ending injuries. Well, hopefully. If you consider your child today, is there anything that you know is off limits today? That you feel like you know you cannot bring that up without feeling the wrath or getting complete avoidance? Many times, it is because there is an emotional bomb tied to whatever the topic is. Respect the boundaries, but I want you to keep in mind that I want you to become MacGyver. You are going to become an expert at diffusing the bombs.

Always be aware of staying within proper boundaries during communication with your child, because you don't want to create offense or eliminate the platform to discuss everything. Obviously, you may have your own set of boundaries, and I am not ignorant to that. We are all also a work in progress. The conversations we may struggle with as father's may be quite easy or relatable in terms of situations that only women experience. I don't give you permission to make your child feel awkward or uncomfortable. Respect hard boundaries. In times where the situation may not require you or you feel a hard boundary, it is quite simple to let them know you are there for them and you respect them. But, make sure someone is openly communicating with them. You cannot afford to miss chances to show them you care. That is the stuff the best dads are made of.

TRFC Pillars

Whole heartedly, I believe there are four major pillars in every relationship. The acronym for the pillars are TRFC. Trust, respect, forgiveness, and commitment. In the content to come, I have dedicated individual chapters just to those subjects and how I see them playing a role in every relationship. When each of these topics are given the proper attention and effort, all relationships thrive. I view trust as the way we bond and how we work to create strong relationships. Respect is essential in the way we interact with one another and how we consider other thoughts, experiences, and feelings. Forgiveness is for all our shortcomings and the mistakes we can so naturally make. Commitment is the glue that holds everything together when we need to be reminded of the person we love and to never give up. All of these elements together held mutually with anyone you deem worthy of your love, create a wonderful and challenging experience to know what life is truly about. Your relationships matter. And why not try to make the best of all of them. My personal belief is that we have an innate desire to relate to the ones we love on a deeper level. It is not the quantity, but the quality of our bonds that define the life we lead. When you consider the relationships you value most, you will easily find the truth in what I am saying. I have tested this theory for years through countless conversations and interactions with people. There is no secondary topic that I have found in any relationship that doesn't have roots back to one of those four main elements. So, keep those in mind as you communicate with any of the people you profess to love. In every decision you make, keep them in mind.

Tone

The tone you use in any conversation, whether written or spoken, automatically signals to the other person what your intentions are. Unless you text everything in all caps because you didn't turn off your caps lock. Then someone may think you are yelling at them to take out the trash. I am sure there are countless stories to be told involving miscommunication. We can create unbelievable misunderstanding if we are not careful even in the way we approach a simple situation. Humans can be quite complicated like that. What may start out as a very simple conversation can go awry when we verbally respond in an uncertain manner. Tone in our voice can influence our perceived understanding. For a very basic example, if you just finished a story to one of your closest friends, and the reaction at the end was a gasp, you know for sure, the ending was quite surprising. If you speak with someone and you notice that they speak in a more somber tone, you may pick up that they may not be feeling well or be sad. What I am telling you is important because later in the book I want you to be able to hear the voice of your child and know exactly when something is going on in their life, so that you don't miss any opportunity. It is possible. Any good welder or any good tradesman in any business can listen to the frequency or tone of their work and easily identify when the quality of what is being produced is favorable. Most welders will tell you that when you weld and it sounds like bacon frying in a pan, you have a good weld. You must trust your ears with your children, because their future depends on it.

Time

It has been said that time is of the essence, and I am still not sure what that means…. I say, it is the most important commodity you have. I know that football game is awesome, and that deadline is coming up. But there are also more important things that need your time and attention. Time drives priorities and priorities drive the experience of that time. Time is of course a human concept as the world around us degrades into the abyss. Well, maybe not that dark, but you get the point. There are countless songs, movies, and schedules dedicated to this unexplainable construct. You can't make more of it, but you can make the most of it. There are unbelievable amounts of efforts, theories, and philosophies that attempt to describe it and understand the true depths of what time means. Fringe physicists and scientists today are still motivated to consider time travel and the application of such magnanimous ideas, because of the complexity and depth of the subject.

Maybe one day, we will be able to time travel, but for now, it is only in the movies and in our memories. Memories serve as a very important tool for life. Memories are the cherished moments created by time and experience that allow us to create long lasting relationships to reflect upon and opportunities to consider for the future. And those memories can help us safeguard our lives and can also help us to find healing in painful situations.

Time can be used in relationships to convey trust, respect, forgiveness, and commitment. For example, trust can be conveyed through time as we demonstrate patience in the lives of our children as they make mistakes or are learning a new skill. Patience is incredibly important in the life of a child, especially from their father. A father who shows no patience and pushes his children forcibly through an opportunity to learn completely neglects nurturing their understanding and is at risk of making the child feel like a failure. A child that is raised to believe they're a failure positions them for the need to overcome much more than as if they had been given permission to make mistakes by a father who so gently loved them. Confidence and assertion grow in the soil of a heart that has been watered with courage and has felt the warmth of patience.

I can specifically remember many times as a father where I didn't use time wisely as a communication tool. I rushed my children to feel the need to be better at something automatically. I had compared them to myself but had failed to compare myself to them. And that's about as disrespectful as you can be. If respect means to regard, I failed. One of the worst feelings a child can feel is disappointment from their father. Don't ever misuse disappointment. I must believe the men and women I've seen use disappointment as a manipulation tactic to create control and superiority, are sadly mistaken and most likely learned this behavior from their father. But time is on my side and yours to help us get it right; for now.

Time allows you the opportunity for forgiveness. Forgiveness can be quite the process depending on the level of pain experienced. But time allows for your perseverance, patience, and persistence to make things right. So, it's important to not misuse it. I know time is a form of communication for forgiveness by just thinking of my late grandfather. I loved him more than most people I've ever met in my life. We had one of the greatest friendships. As an adult, I couldn't be in the same room without him telling heartfelt stories of me as a child and I never grew tired of them. He loved me and he never let me think different for a second. But as close as we were, I was always slightly bothered or at least didn't understand why, if I hadn't called him or stopped by in a couple of weeks, he would always say to me the next time I saw him, "boy, I thought I've done something wrong." I didn't like it. In a way, it made me feel like he was forcing me to feel guilty. But that was never his intentions, it was just the way he communicated his love. He passed away over four years ago, and I would give anything to hear him say that now. I would no longer feel any self-imposed guilt, but I would happily give him the best hug a grandson could. So, use your time not only wisely, but also with words.

Environment

We must work to eliminate the misconception that we don't need to express the way we feel. Not sharing yourself with your children is also a form of communication; a very poor one. I've spoken with many people that are so hungry for a better relationship with their father that I cannot afford to not bring it up. At times in my own life, my children have told me that they never knew how I felt or if I even noticed some of the things that were going on in their lives. And that was quite an eye opener to me, as I felt fairly connected. And to boot, those comments were made at times when I was only working a standard 40-hour work week. I'm sure they felt even more separated from me when I was working 80-100 hours a week. But that's the way it is most of the time as we can be quite delusional in our efforts to provide for our family. There's no shame in working hard, providing, or even setting goals for yourself. But my target for this book is to help you build a foundation and framework for a healthy relationship with the best communication and best balance possible. I want you to be able to know that when you grow old, you did your best in the most valuable role ever given to you.

If you pause and think back to when you were young, I hope that you can find happy memories. There are times in our lives when we revisit the physical places we've been and recall the very specific way we felt in that space. I've been able to visit places in the world that I can only describe as a living painting. For example, when you come out of the tunnel and see Yosemite Valley for the first time, it's quite difficult to put into words what you feel. Yes, you see trees, mountains, and waterfalls. But, it's so much more than that. It emotionally leaves you in awe. And that same fundamental nature is what we must work to capture in the relationship with our children. I want them to say that you're not just a dad, your so much more. I want you to be able to create awe and wonder in their life. Create an environment that inspires them. Be their living painting. Know that the environment that you create for them is influential in how they interact with the world around them. Your environmental influence you provide comes back as a long-term communication to your children in the form of memories. When you give them your time, you make it possible for them to think. When you give them your kindness, you make it possible for them to feel safe and able to speak. When you give them your love, you teach them to believe.

Relate

Find ways to relate to your children. Oh, but my children are much different than I was, or they are too old for that now. Don't make excuses. Consider them, no matter what age they are. Sympathy is when you can relate to someone because you care. Empathy is when you relate to someone because you have shared in similar or like experiences. Maybe you don't know what it's like to be a 13-year-old girl adjusting to middle school, but I can assure you she would do much better going through it if she knew someone put forth an effort to be there for her. Maybe you don't know what it's like to lose a job or a home, but your adult child who may be enduring one of the hardest times of their life does. Find a way to bring comfort. Maybe you don't have the exact answers, but find ways to relate, even if it means doing something outside of your comfort zone. Being an excuse maker is not a good look for a father. He really must be more of a way maker. Being relatable is half the battle when it comes to relationships. It communicates that you understand or at least are giving an effort to understand. You can't always fix the problem, but you can put forth an effort to relate. In my fatherly experience, I cannot say I have ever run short on opportunities to relate. When you reflect, I am sure you feel the same way. Time after time our children look to us to help them. When they fall, they want you to not only help them up, but to also find a band aid and kiss their boo boo's. The real objective is for you to understand that it was a painful experience for them. No different than when they go through their first heartbreak. Never turn a blind eye to your children. Don't give them the discount version of yourself by missing the chance to show them you care. Relationships grow cold when you don't pay attention to the needs of the other person.

Six years ago, my mother was diagnosed with thyroid cancer. After her diagnosis, her doctor informed her that the cancer was a rare form that was genetic. He immediately advised that she let her children know that they must be tested for the gene and proceed with removal of the thyroid if they were positive for the mutation. Because if they were, the doctor stated there was a ninety nine percent chance they could develop the cancer and there would be no treatment available. Well, I was positive for the gene and had a thyroidectomy shortly after the prognosis. I was really upset with the situation. I had my own personal training business and I also had been in the best shape of my life. I couldn't believe this was happening to me. I went through denial and was upset that my kids unknowingly could also carry this same gene. It wasn't my mother's fault and I wasn't upset with her.

If anything, I was completely grateful to her, because for the first year after she found out, she spent it pushing me to have the surgery. My denial was strong. Almost too strong, but she persisted in her persuasion and trying to relate to me as she had gone through the same thing. I believe that is what helped me the most to have it done. And it was just in time, because afterwards, the doctor told me that my cells in my thyroid had already began negatively changing.

Fast forward a couple of years and two of my five children tested positive for the gene. I wrestled again with having a thyroid removed, just not my own. I had made up my mind that I would wait until they were eighteen and they could decide for themselves. Mainly, because it was extremely difficult for me to adjust to my new life without a thyroid. I was lethargic, I had anxiety, stress, and I just couldn't focus. These were all things I had never experienced before. Frankly, I couldn't imagine putting my children through that. Like most people, I can be quite stubborn or set in my ways when I conclude a thought in my mind. That all changed when I met my new endocrinologist who challenged my thinking and asked me to consider the fact that this cancer had been detected as early as age five in children. And he told me it would be far better to allow them to deal with the short-term struggle of no thyroid than battle cancer. That insight and his compassion combined caused me to reconsider my stance. But what stuck with me the most was his careful appeal to me. I was quite clear with the doctor about my decision, but he met me with the same energy. I will never forget what he said as he doubled down. He told me that my children would be in great hands with me as their father, because I could relate to them. I could walk out this journey right alongside them. Helping them to make it through what I knew wouldn't be easy, simply inspired me. He helped me to see that my valued communication to my children is that I've been there, and I understand. I know the struggles, but I will help you and I will be here for you on your journey and I am forever grateful to him. And he was right, I have been right here, holding their hands all along the way. By that change of my decisions, I have truly found that relating to your children is one of the greatest forms of communication you can provide.

Balance

Find every opportunity to listen to your child. There are times when you feel the need to speak, but there are moments when you must set aside your need to just "fix" situations. The core of the relationship with our children requires us to hear them out in every situation. There are times where I find myself being overly protective or not able to see the big picture. My kids can wake me up from that when I need it most. Balance is important because it is rooted in trust and respect. When we show them that we are willing to consider what they have to say or their very actions, we strengthen the relationship; even if they fail at what they attempt. One of the worst forms of parenting is when we fall back into the "because I said so's". That is not safe territory for healthy development. You can be the sole decision maker, but you could also give your family the opportunity to speak in unison with compromise in the forefront. Balance is key in every wise and well thought out decision we make as individuals. I applaud families who take into consideration the opinions and notions of other members of the family concerning their direction in life.

When my wife and I were contemplating having another child, we had to consider that our youngest was seven, we were in our mid 30's, and what the other kids thought about the idea. Of course, it was family meeting time. The initial conversation started with, "what do you guys think about having another little brother or sister?" They weren't exactly excited about the idea and the conversation suddenly changed into asking "why are you guys not ok with this?" Totally not what we anticipated as an outcome. We gave it some more time and let them really think about what we were asking. We brought it up a few weeks later and the responses were better or at least more favorable to having a new sibling. We decided as a family that it would now be a good idea to have a new family member.

Eventually, we had a baby on the way. So, we thought. Turns out, it was two. So, we had twice the celebration in our home because of how we discussed our new addition in proper balance and consideration of everyone in the home. I really don't think they would have been as excited if they hadn't been part of the discussion. That respect is not always given and for you that may seem farfetched to include your children in the conversation. But if you are to move cohesively into the future, you need the input from everyone. Hard feelings can come over the simplest things. It is important for you to stay on top of every situation and really develop an understanding of not only how you feel, but also how everyone else in the home feels. That simple consideration will take you so much further in life by making the choice to include.

Chapter 2 | Trust

Long-lasting stress, pressure, and impact are created continually in the life of a child always jockeying for the position of trust and belief with their father. It's quite difficult to fully explain this desire for pride from our fathers, but one major element is in knowing that our fathers trust us. How much more powerful is it when a father can take away the mystery and let his children know you have their trust right out of the gate, regardless of failures or victories? Is it even possible? Can you do it, are you up to task? I think this is an extremely challenging area for men but can be quite dynamic if unleashed in the life of any child. A child will happily throw inhibition to the wind when we have cleared them from the looming pressure of our approval. When we provide our children with immediate, selfless trust, we disarm the need for them to focus on making us proud and they instinctively operate in complete liberty.

Most of our daily decisions are based on life experiences that still continue to shape our worldview and also from what we received in the form of belief from our parents. Maybe you remember jumping into the water for the first time as a child with your parents urging you on. Some kids may have been excited, but some may have been afraid. But it's not about the emotions, it's about the trust. You look out at the water, which is much bigger than you and is much deeper than your perceived ability to swim and you subconsciously question the very trust you have in this person to know that they are going to help you if you need them.

Also consider when we learn to walk, it is typically with the guidance of our parents. From that age, we may not have the capacity of memory to recall the moment, but I can assure you at that time, there was an element of trust involved. So, down to the very first steps in life, a child must learn to trust their parent. I know that may not be your story or situation, but for right now, I want to speak to the very basic concepts. The good news is that your child, no matter what age, is still learning to walk and your trust matters to them on every step of their entire journey. Below I am going to expound different ideas concerning the types of trust and how they are applied in our relationships.

Given trust

A child generally trusts his or her parents freely and naturally. You can see trust in the body language of a child. When you see a young child hide behind or cling to the legs of their parent, you know this is a child who emulates the core demonstration of trust. A child looks to their father as a provider and protector and those are the reasons in which the trust thrives. When a child knows you will do everything in your power to assure them that they are safe and without need, you solidify the most important natural instincts they have, which ultimately make them feel accepted. As a child grows, that trust is given out more and more. Every positive interaction provided allows them the knowledge and experience they need to become the greatest versions of themselves.

If you look back into your past, your closest friendships and relationships involve a couple of often overlooked attributes. One of them being, who can help you keep your secrets. Why is that so important? Because, trust is important. While they may not necessarily be bad or good secrets, we've allowed someone into the intimate portions of our life. One of the other ways people get into our automatic trust zone besides keeping our secrets, is by defending us without second thought. Let's look at this scenario. Suppose your child is sitting in class at school and another kid aggressively pushes them out of the desk. Your child's best friend is sitting next to them and their response is to laugh at them as it happens. And perhaps another random child stands up and pushes the aggressor away in a moment's notice. Who do you suppose your child will place their trust in for future experiences like this? And who do you think your child will be most likely to try and create a more genuine friendship with? Possibly, one friendship ends, and another begins, because of one action and one subject that just so happens to be an extremely powerful tool in terms of bonding and relationship building.

Take every opportunity to establish and develop trust in the life of your child. When a child feels that they can't count on you or that you cannot keep your word, the relationship will begin to falter. A child is extremely long suffering and has a great capacity for forgiveness, but as that child ages to a young adult, the damage can be almost certainly irreversible. And, I can't promise everything will ever get back to good, but it is important to never give up on our most important relationships. A father always takes the first steps when it comes to giving trust. As strong as a child's trust may be, we cannot afford to misplace it or not understand the real tremendous value. For your child to navigate life, they are going to really need to be able to count on you and the level of trust they have in you.

When my oldest daughter was going through middle school, obviously the dating conversation came up. Our relationship regarding trust was fairly solid. My very first dating advice was simply this – purely mathematical, "If there are four boys and four girls in your class and three of the other girls have boyfriends, that last boy is not your boyfriend by default." Let me point out the first lesson wasn't about how I automatically didn't trust her, it was to let her know, I am for you and not against you. I don't know much about dating these days, but I know sometimes kids can be forced into situations that aren't about trust at all, but social pressure. And it just gets more intense for them in social situations as time goes on. But raise strong kids that have a network of people that trust them to make the right decisions. By talking about it the way I did, I allowed her to see that I completely trusted her, and my intention was to give her sound and simple ideas. The worst thing you can do is attack your child and make them feel alone because you don't trust them or even try to.

One day you may walk your daughter down the aisle or be your son's best man, or maybe you already have. This is again an act of trust. If I know that my father has my best interest at hand, he won't purposefully allow me to make a mistake with someone I am making one of the largest commitments of my life. Yes, I know sometimes kids don't listen, but don't forget, sometimes, we aren't fully engaged either. And blame has no place in the relationship of a father and his children. If you guide your children in a way that allows them to make mistakes, but also give them correction when they need it, they will value your insight and opinion more than anyone else. The true power of a good Father is not in the strength of direction he gives, but in the ways, he looks to serve and guide his children. If your child trusts you, your influence is never in question and your guidance is always welcome.

Maybe children have misguided ideas about life, but that is where your opportunity for creativity lies. Take advantage of the small talk, because that is where all big ideas start. For most people, meaningful small talk only occurs with the ones we truly trust. How much we share determines how much we trust in many cases. If you feel like the relationship is not accessible, maybe it is time to revisit what may be hindering the trust. Openness, honesty and vulnerability are the three main chords on the guitar of real naturally given trust. We often protect our weak spots and guard our sensitivity for reasons of self-preservation. But in the presence of the person or people we trust, we can relax. We experience safety, security, and freedom to talk openly and most importantly, be ourselves.

Earned trust

If you and your child are looking for a car on their sixteenth birthday, chances are, you aren't going to go get the 500 HP dragster for the back and forth commute for school. Because you most likely have considered the amount of experience they have driving and their full decision-making abilities regarding the highway and "the need for speed". After all, we are talking about something that could easily take the life of the one you love. You would most likely consider a vehicle that would be decent, affordable, and safe. Our children's order of priorities may be that it looks cool and drives fast. Ignore their begging and stick to your guns. Great opportunities to provide earned trust are just around the corner. After reasonable time and good behavior, other options may be considered, totally your call. Nonetheless, these are golden opportunities that place power directly in the palm of your hand. So, how does that work? If a child has a car, this item contains power. It is up to you how you choose to control and administer that power. The leverage is in your favor, but don't abuse or misuse it. In terms of earned trust, you must give them the chance to prove they can both manage what they've been given, no matter what it is. And if you rules and recommendations are not followed, simply move the fulcrum point towards you.

I am not one who believes in giving my child everything they ask for. Years ago, we bought into the idea of giving our children allowances for completed chores and did so for a while. But we realized later that we were potentially setting ourselves up for failure later down the road. I was causing my children to look to my wife and I as their source for things that needed to be done regardless of pay. We readjusted our thinking to consider their responsibility in the house, not under the merit of money, but under the merit of trust. If they couldn't take care of the small things they were given, I couldn't establish a way to trust them with the larger things later in life. We put it back in perspective and focused on the things that mattered.

In some parts of the world, we are inundated with stuff. Almost to the point, that we forget to live our lives based on simple principles and ideals. You may not be able to pay your child in trust, but the ROI is through the roof. When you ask them to clean their room or rake the leaves without pay, they quickly realize there is something more to life than stuff and money. That doesn't mean they appreciate it now, but they will. They may not always keep their room clean or do everything you ask, but you must stay the course. You are not paying an employee; you are raising children to be responsible for what they have. Remind them of that. Don't set your children up for failure and paint dreams for them as if they are freely given or are easy to attain. Teach them what hard work looks like; demonstrate it. Don't just bark out orders, get your own hands dirty as well. You only have a very short amount of time to solidify those bonds with your children. Yes, hard work will take you far in life, but you also need opportunities to get you there. While you can, push them to take on the hard work, and you take care of the opportunities. Allow them to earn your trust and reward them. But not just with things. Your time is much more valuable. After all, the main idea of this book is to balance being a Working Class Dad. But also, keep in mind, it's not only about them earning your trust, you need to earn theirs.

As a child comes of age, they think more clearly and even question if you are trustworthy or even care about them at all. Do you study your child? Are you involved in the details they share with you? Can you remember the last big thing they shared with you? Every time you don't, you are chipping away at that trust and your connectivity weakens. You can earn a child's trust most by just listening to them. They may appreciate your opinion, advice, or even your guidance, but they also want to be heard. From a father's perspective, we are looking at earned trust from a state of knowing that our children can interact with the world without harming themselves or causing harm to others. For a child, they are looking at it from terms of still establishing bonds and navigating the world. You've already gained some understanding for this stage of your life, but please don't forget that they haven't. It could be quite a dangerous mistake if you overlook the importance.

Don't forget that the other side of the coin for earned trust is keeping your word. Disappointment is the destructive hammer that shatters the delicate glass vase of expectations. Make every excuse possible to keep your commitments to your children over anything else that you think matters right now. If you lose a promotion because you kept your word to your children, it doesn't matter. It may bother you today, but don't forget, being a father is far more important than anything else. From one father to another – get your priorities in order! I've spent far too much time trying to make on time deliveries to and for people who could care less about the individual impact and the personal consequences affecting another human being. Not to say they are bad people, but this is the danger of a "business as usual" attitude. Be aggressive and dogmatic in the way you pursue the heart of your children. Stay true to your own passions and desires, but not at the cost of losing everything that matters. Don't forget that your consistency is vital to the development and sustainability of the relationship.

Broken trust

Traditional trust in business by way of handshakes and verbal agreements are considered by the majority of businessman as almost nonexistent and comical in today's culture. I have heard many businessmen say on the eve of finalizing a great deal, "I will believe it when the money is in the bank." Or for myself, I have had experiences in business firsthand that make me believe the handshake is dead. The disappointment of broken trust is hard to get over. I'm sure if you were to go back even 40 years ago, you would find a much different culture than now. Not to say that we are worse off, but when people are "burned" or have felt the pain of broken trust, they come up with ways to not let it happen again. Hence, contracts, non competes, and NDA's. Life is very similar when we have let down the ones we love or have truly disappointed them. Avoidance, unavailability, and absence take over the relationship. Solitude and singularity are not great for relationships, but easy to do when you have grown tired of disappointment.

I recently sat next to a gentleman in first class on a flight to San Jose and we immediately struck up a conversation. It's noteworthy that he was fairly intoxicated. However, being almost eighty years old, his appearance was quite polished. He wore silver slick backed hair, a clean shave, and was dressed the part. His Rolex and gold bracelet were quite remarkable. His Louis Vuitton bag had a special status tag hanging on that read 2-Million-mile club for this specific airline carrier. I could tell he meant business. Whatever he had done with his life, he seemed quite successful based on appearance and financially speaking. He was intriguing and I wanted to know more. I went automatically into reporter mode asking shallow questions but eventually building up to what I really wanted to find out and that is how he lived his life in on the inside. Maybe a personal flaw on my part, but you can't help what interests you. He informed me that he made his millions by owning car dealerships and selling airplanes. I saw photos of himself and certain celebrities on his phone and the photo of his Lamborghini; which is one of my favorite cars. He even told me, "don't worry, you will have one, one day." We'll see. I was feeling quite overwhelmed and skeptical with such a fantastical personality and then he continued to tell me how he recently donated a jet to an aviation museum. At this point, I was leaning towards the celebrities being impersonators and the Lamborghini photo being him just leaning up against a random car. Then he pulled a magazine from his bag and highlighted the actual photo of the plane and him. The title read, "Local businessman donates jet to aviation museum." I had no choice but to believe what he said now. He had more than actual photos to back up these previously unvalidated and audacious statements. He had what appeared to be a legitimate publication. But again, another lesson in trust. We don't just give it out – case in point. It doesn't mean we are bad people, just guarded. But, now to the real point. After all the talk of "success" and the quotes from him like "Get it while its hot", and "work hard, play harder", I got down to business. "What was your biggest regret?", I asked him. I must admit, I wasn't quite ready. He teared up and said he regretted putting his work ahead of his family. It caused him to lose everything that truly mattered. He said his children hated him for what he did to their mother and what he put their family through. He said it was the main reason he was a self-admitted drunk today. He had promised his kids repeatedly that he would quit drinking, but he said that he just couldn't do it. He was quite ashamed when he shared with me that his son was picking him up at the airport that day and he knew he would be disappointed in him once again. From a man who had spent the first hour talking about success in business, he spent the second hour in shambles. He explained that a hospital room when you're just out of surgery from a malignant tumor removal was like hell on earth when you realize no one is there waiting to see you. He had cancer earlier that year and was still going through treatments. He said not having the people there he loved the most was worse than the cancer. He told me not to take my children for granted and to make sure I loved my wife with everything I had. I will never forget him telling me to not make the same mistakes. That level of broken, I had never seen before. It is quite strange how our perception of some people can get rocked to the core, by just a little small talk. He may have been one of the most financially wealthy people I have ever spoken with, but rest assured he was also one of the most relationally impoverished individuals I have ever met as well. I struggled to provide real words of encouragement for him.

From a business perspective, he said something that stuck with me as well. I also asked him how did he accumulate his wealth? Not in terms of strategy, but in terms of mindset. He explained that he never cared if he made a dime, he just knew he wanted to be successful, no matter what. That conversation helped me to put my own life under the microscope. Is there anything I'd be willing to lose everything for? You bet, and I identified that as my family. Very few things in life I have found that I would give all for. I am sure I am not alone in this thinking. With every decision for a father, you always have an opportunity to count the cost. He told me also that he was always able to give them everything they asked for materialistically, even their own businesses. But missed out on the chance to give them the love and attention they needed. Years of breaking their trust had compounded into a life of emotional misery. He clung to the alcohol to deal with the pain. Broken trust is unbelievably difficult to overcome. But, if this is you, and you think it's too late; it's not. Love never gives up and love never fails. Maybe you need to make some personal changes or adjustments to what you are willing to accept. But don't give up. Reconciliation takes time and involves a ravenous pursuit of the ones we love.

Redistributed trust

When your relationships are in shambles and it feels as if hope may be lost, you still have options. No matter where you are in the relationship you want to seek to rebuild, it won't be easy. There is no easy way. You must retrace your steps and find the root of what went wrong. You must ask yourself how bad you want it and how committed to the resolution you are. If your children have lost full faith in you because of events that caused them harm or if it's because you may have directly harmed them, you will need to start small. If you have been legally separated, I don't advise breaking the law. And in no way am I advocating that you put your child in a situation that is too much for them to bear because of overwhelming emotional or physical harm you may have caused them. I am fully aware that there are some relationships out there that are better off left alone.

In the same way, I counsel my children regarding marriage or any friendship, they should never put up with physical or mental abuse – zero tolerance. If this was your situation, I would suggest seeking legal consultation about how to proceed and I wish you the best. But in cases where both parties are communicable and amicable, I suggest starting slow. Reach out to your children in a way that you expect nothing in return. Own your failures. Communicate in a way that puts their needs ahead of yours. Request their guidance for feedback and solutions that can allow you to rebuild the relationship. They ultimately have the responsibility to redistribute the trust. But it won't be an easy process. It is going to take hard work. Maybe even going to a professional counselor together.

If your children have broken your trust. Take the first steps towards reconciliation. Do all you can with every opportunity to make things right. I understand that our children can make very bad decisions and you reserve the right to offer forgiveness and redistribute trust. But when you consider life and how many people are willing to just throw anyone to the side as invaluable or damaged goods, that is never the intended role of a father. I again strongly suggest starting early with the right value system and prioritizing a healthy relationship to supplementally manage conflicts in the future. But even that's not enough at times, sometimes you have got to dig deep. If necessary, may you always be the one to stand in the rain outside your child's front door to let them know you are here and that you will never give up on them. It may take time for progress to appear, but I can assure you that no child ever truly rejects their father's genuine effort, commitment and dedication to them, not for long anyways.

Chapter 3 | Respect

No matter how young or old an individual is, we have a humanitarian requirement to consider what that person thinks, feels, or has to say. Several years ago, I stopped by the mall on the way home from work to buy my wife a few of her favorite hand soaps at Bath and Body Works. I hurriedly went in, picked out a few and exited the store. Upon exiting, my attention was drawn to an elderly woman in a wheelchair who was leaning over from her chair almost in a strain to reach for a mother and a baby that were passing in front of her. The mother was holding the tiny new infant in a mobile car seat and seemed to be leaning away from her with reluctance. The older woman's body language seemed to be quite desperate in the way she reached out, almost as if for help, but with an intense glare in her eyes. Time stood still as I watched this woman reach her frail hand out to this infant who appeared to have something she needed. The mother must have realized this as well as she decided to lean back to the elderly woman and allow her to see the baby. I witnessed a faint grin grow across her face as her aged hand touched the hand of youth. Although what I witnessed comes across as a sweet or considerate moment, it was not the way I felt when I first saw the interaction about to take place, and I don't think the young mother did either. It felt awkward and inconvenient. Especially for people who are constantly in a hurry. Sort of like when a father is trying to rush out the door and one of the little ones are trying to hang on to our feet… But when I departed and walked out of the main entrance of the mall, I noticed a nursing home van parked out front and that is when it hit me. I got to my car and sat down. Immediately, I thought about this moment and how it had probably been ages since this elderly woman even touched a baby. I realized that in the hustle and bustle of our everyday life it is so easy to overlook and not give the proper regard to the situations or people we so frequently encounter. And to be regarded is the very heart of respect. And isn't that what all of us really want?

The best way to communicate with a small child is to get down to eye level, because they feel understood and connected. The opponent to eye level communication is where the phrase you've heard "talking down to someone" literally comes from. Therefore, it is extremely important to keep in mind positionally how you speak with your children. Standing over someone can be viewed as aggressive and intimidating behavior. Look to nature for the confirmation in that statement. Intimidated animals' stoop and bow down to animals who push for height over them in confrontational situations. Often turning belly up to show that they are not a threat. But the great thing is you are not an animal and you can control how you interact with others. You can make choices with body language just the same as the very tone and level of your voice.

A father must always lead with respect in mind. Intimidation and screaming at a child are an incredibly lazy way of parenting. In our normal workday, we don't interact by screaming at our colleagues or customers. If you do, I highly suggest counseling. Once, as a manager, I called a meeting with twelve guys in whom

I was responsible for. There had been some back and forth arguments about work that needed to be completed, but suddenly it turned personal. Words were exchanged between two of them that just so happened to be quite good friends. I felt that the only way to find resolve was to bring everyone together and get everything out in the open with civility. I was a new manager at the time, but had a real belief, and still do, that people just really want to be heard. These were all grown men who had families and children and real responsibilities. We went through the meeting and all issues were discussed, and all were resolved. Afterwards, I noticed two of my same level managers that were in attendance, stay behind after everyone left. They immediately criticized me for being nice and trying to hear the guys out. They told me you can't speak to these people like that because the only thing they understood was to be yelled at. I immediately felt sad for these two men and their children, and their viewpoints of the world. Regardless of their views, listening to my guys allowed me to build some of the best working relationships. I knew them all on a personal level and made it a point to give them the respect they needed, regardless of any position or title I could have thought made me better than them. And the same for my managerial colleagues, even though we had very different management styles, I still had no hard feelings. We are all at different levels of maturity and are completely pure works in progress. You may look at a forty-year-old man and see a forty-year-old man, but when you look in his eyes and get to know the real person, you may quickly find that he is only eight or nine years old mentally.

And that's why a father must offer respect to his children for the sake of proper development in areas of self-worth, acceptance, understanding, and tolerance.

Personal Respect

This type of respect is the reservoir of fireworks we carry in our soul. The very substance we live and die for. Our passion and dignity abide there. When you find the truth that is within you, you can't ignore it. If a child has a father who can help draw it out, that child has a major advantage in life. For example, some children look to the sky, see a plane and say automatically that they want to be a pilot. Some look to the sky, see a plane, and say I am afraid of heights. And by that example, I am reminded of Neil Armstrong. His father was taking him up in planes and allowing him to fly long before most kids ever got behind the steering wheel of a car. He believed in him. He saw something that was driving his son to learn how to fly. And as you know, Neil went on to be the first man to walk on the moon. Whatever personal conviction or internal regard Neil had, his father found a way to get it out of him and make it become reality. That same personal conviction, regard, and ambition is what your child has within them. Maybe not to walk on the moon, but completely special and spectacular to them. So much so, that it can't be just brushed aside. What a child believes about themselves, they will become. That personal respect must be developed to allow them to achieve. Otherwise, they will rarely be able to stand up for what they believe.

I have seen personal respect demonstrated in the workplace on many occasions. One of the most impactful, was when a former colleague in a leadership development program was nearing the end and decided to opt out. He decided he didn't want to pursue the next steps into management. Chris was the kind of guy that everyone respected because of his work ethic, honesty, and natural leadership abilities. But in some companies, it's not about your unique qualities or abilities at all, but rather about what they can persuade you to become. And managers are forced to use a proverbial mold with the pointed objective of producing a certain type of leader. And because guys like him carry strong personal respect and dignity, they can't squelch who they naturally are, so they just don't fit the mold. Like Chris, I hope my children wouldn't forsake their authenticity if ever faced with that as well. I don't mean in radical terms of anarchy or complete nonconformists, but in the sense that they don't compromise for anything less than being true to themselves.

Regarding the development of personal respect, it's mandatory to put your children first. The medium is time. They need to know that it is excellent to consider the things that fascinate them, and they should be encouraged to pursue them. Strive to avoid the cookie cutter mentality that they must be just like you, like the same things you do, and share the same opinions as you. If you crush their authenticity, you are not fathering, but reinforcing the broadly accepted corporate mentality that awaits them. And by focusing on them and their genuine interests, you can help them avoid some major unwarranted disappointments. It would probably be quite surprising to most parents out there that our children really don't want to play certain sports we enroll them in or play a part in a play just because you did. It's not personal. But it's important to consider. Our individuality develops in our personal respect for ourselves. Our personal respect helps us in our everyday decision-making abilities. We set our boundaries internally also from our experiences and interactions with the world.

Our largest contribution to how we see the world takes place in the home where we are raised. When you speak with your children, don't seek to influence them to be exactly like you, but help them to find their own path. Although they may look just like you, they are not you. Allow them to develop into the person they were intended to be. If you have raised your children and they are grown, take time to ask them questions about their time growing up and what they really liked and if they wanted to get anything off their chests. No matter the age of your children, they will appreciate that you respect them enough to ask. Because after all, it shows that you care.

Pivotal Respect

So, in personal respect we observed our ability to define ourselves and help our children. Pivotal respect is how we consider our children and how we teach them to consider others. We must teach our children, no matter what age, to have respect and consideration for all people. The climate we live in today forces us to fight to be in the front of the highest priority line at any and all costs. When pivotal respect is developed it helps us to teach our children to listen more attentively to one another and look to pivot to a point that may be outside of their own minds or experience.

Teaching your child the value of listening may be a bit of a lost art. Partially, because the normal daily interaction is something like this – Little Tommy goes to public school. He sits down in his class. His cell phone is buzzing with texts and he is checking social media. The distractions are unlimited. He comes home with a bad grade. Dad yells at him. Dad gets back on social media or to his distracting object of affection. Repeat. Sad story, but I can guarantee you it happens every day in abundance. Now, distractions and passing the buck on responsibilities have left you in a poor situation to teach your son the real value of listening. To have at least half a chance, you must be involved with them. And it's not just about listening for the sake of learning at school, it's also about learning in life.

One interaction worth mentioning this year is a story that I recently heard about from a friend. She shared with me that her son was sitting at the middle school lunch table by two boys who were a couple of seats away and an altercation took place. One of them threw ketchup at the other and then he proceeded to tell him to go now and get napkins to clean up the mess. So, it wasn't just enough to throw ketchup on him, he now was barking orders at him to clean it up. And not forgetting to mention that the kids at the table were all laughing at him and he was completely embarrassed. My friend shared this because she was disturbed that her child was one of the kids laughing at the victim. Social pressure is extremely difficult to navigate for both children and adults. But if this pivotal respect isn't taught and we don't learn how to properly consider others, we create even worse societal problems. We lose the ability to show sympathy or common concern for others. There was a notable incident in recent years where a gentleman fell from a pier and drown as several teenagers recorded him struggling in choppy water. They was laughter on the video and never one mention of making any effort to save him. A society without sympathy for one another is a very dangerous society. We cannot afford to miss opportunities that demonstrate or help our child develop common pivotal respect for others. To pivot means to not just consider yourself but be moved to think consider others. When my friend asked her son what he thought the little boy who had ketchup thrown was feeling, he immediately realized the error of his ways. He hadn't considered that it was embarrassing or what he would have done if this happened to him. He told her that the vice principal did come over at the end and take both boys away to his office. But it didn't stop him or his friends to think collectively about what happened on a deeper level. I can vividly remember a similar situation in high school, and it didn't end so well. The entire lunchroom table was cleared out and a huge brawl pursued. All because the line had been crossed between two friends. Respect causes us to draw hard boundaries for what we are willing to entertain. If we can take the time to teach our children about respect for not only themselves, but for others and what they may be facing, we are doing our best.

So, we win in two ways; it does not create regret for us and in turn communicates thoughtfulness, understanding, and tolerance for other human beings in the mind and heart of your children.

It is important for fathers to consider the way their children feel in various situations as well. When you speak with them, they can tell what you really think and if you understand the way they feel. Or maybe it's not so extreme. Maybe your child just feels like you don't have time for them, and it turns into a "nothing fight". A nothing fight is when too much time and space come between any relationship and tension is elevated because of the unspoken frustrations. A young lady in her twenties named Emily I sat next to on a plane to Charlotte shared her own personal nothing fight story with me. She shared with me that she was recently married and had a wonderful husband and a new home and lived a couple of hours away from her parents. She said she had been out of her parents' home for a couple of years now but had since stopped communicating with her father. Every time she called home, her father answered the phone and would immediately hand it to her mother, as if he had no time for her. It was confusing and heartbreaking for her. Nothing happened between them, he just became distant over time. I could tell it was extremely difficult as she shed tears on the plane. Our conversation was one that needed to take place. It's not every day you can open up to someone who is going to really listen and not give you a partial opinion about what may or may not be going on. She had my full respect as I considered what she was going through. It didn't mean I had a solution for her or would even offer to fix it. But at least I wanted her to know someone cared enough to listen. Many times, the solution is already in your own mind, if you just have another person to help you discover it. She told me the conversation motivated her to end the nothing fights with her father and find a way to get things back to good.

Some of you fathers know this story all too well. There may be no reason at all for this situation, but we didn't take the time to consider how we've made our children feel. You may be busy with work or your hobby and completely overlook what is going on at home. What is truly important is to remember this principal as you communicate with your children. You may feel like it is not your responsibility, but I can assure you that you are wrong. Something may have hurt you but do everything you can to show regard what they are feeling. When you show your consideration for them, it's more than just a lesson, it communicates respect.

Pragmatic respect

Sir, ma'am, thank you, you're welcome and please are all just things tied strongly to my southern raising. Having lived in the north for almost six years now, I can say that I have now relaxed a little. But that doesn't mean I have relaxed completely with my children, especially in the home. I found it quite surprising when we moved north that some people were offended when you used basic pragmatic respect. But societal norms vary from region to region around our very big country. But there are still ways that pragmatic respect stays the same. The value of true pragmatic respect is built into the very core of many of the languages around the world. To the point that you have no option but to address someone in a manner of full respect. We don't always grasp that concept in the US, because of the slang we so often use. Whether it's business or home communication, we have basic expectations to abide by when speaking to one another. Out of any of the accolades or awards my children have ever received, nothing makes happier than when someone recognizes that my child is respectful.

Common decency and courtesy are some of the first things that come to mind. For these, I would have you consider basic things like holding the door open for someone or allowing someone to merge in traffic There was a time in my life that I thought these things happened naturally or without situational consideration, but as I have traveled and had more life experience, I realize logistics can get in the way. In a small town, you may be more apt to hold the door for someone entering. However, in a larger city, you may become the new doorman and get put on salary for the kind gesture. The sheer volume of people entering in can make that a very unrealistic thing to do. It doesn't make the people less appreciative of what you are doing, but it does not fit into the pragmatic sense of respect any longer. It passes into a new unmanageable threshold. So, situationally, we may have to change what we do in certain interactions. My general advice to my children is to take advantage of the opportunities you are given to be kind and show respect for others. But, from my earlier point, it can be quite difficult to define depending on where you live or work or what may be considered normal, so proceed with caution.

In your own mind you may have just read this and thought, "well, that example or situation would have upset me". However, this is the next portion of pragmatic respect and probably the most important. It teaches us tolerance and acceptance when we see the world and realize it as not being in total control of our environment. Other people live here and have their own life experiences that shape who they are. I once had a very close friend whom I held the door open for as we were walking through and he refused to go ahead of me. I was surprised and honestly caught off guard. This guy was an outstanding friend and one of the best people I had met in terms of friendliness. It bothered me and felt offensive that we were at an awkward sort of standoff, because he refused to just walk through the door that I was holding open. I gave in and walked in first and let the door hit him in the head as he followed. Not really, I jest. But I did walk in ahead and went to my office. I thought about that all day before I finally went to him and asked what that was about. His answer surprised me more. He told me that when he was young his father taught him that men never open the door for men. I had never even heard something like this. For a moment, I questioned what I had been taught and if I was wrong for doing it. I questioned my masculinity for a moment. I wondered if I had been taught wrong. I wondered if what I thought was a friendly gesture made other people feel awkward without ever thinking about it. I didn't like this feeling. I am not ashamed to write this down. If anything, it is liberating. Because your children will need to learn the same things. Don't forget that it wasn't that long ago when it was normal for many fathers to not show affection or even verbally express to their children that they love them. I can't define what you accept or teach your children, but I can at least help you to be aware that not everyone may share your individual definition of pragmatic respect.

I am reminded of a conversation my wife and I recently had with a lady who shared a story about her five year old son and how she would allow him to dress up in dresses and wear makeup. For us, there were a few questions. Where did he get this idea and where did he get the dresses? She let us know that he wanted to dress like mommy, and she made it happen. Although we didn't agree, we were understanding and respectful in the situation. My wife shared a few stories with her about our son who was three at the time and who has a twin sister. (Information just for fairness of the story.) My wife told her how our son was complete opposite of his sister. He refused to drink out of any cup that wasn't blue. He did this naturally. He refused to play barbies with his sister. And the lady seemed to be shocked. She asked us if we taught him to be that way. My wife told her of course not, as it was the way he naturally behaved. It doesn't mean either of us are right or wrong about how we choose to parent, but rather we show respect to each other for doing our best in every situation. That conversation may be personal for you or you may feel slightly offended, but keep in mind – that's the point. We must maintain our pragmatic respect for one another and take advantage of teaching our children how to do so as well. Anytime you teach acceptance and tolerance you are making a better world. I can't think of anything better I could ask you to do in a situation like that. If you think condemning the lady on the plane for allowing her son to wear dresses is going to fix anything, you are mistaken. If you want to condemn me for promoting toxic masculinity, you would be wrong for that as well.

Parenting does not mean forcing your child to be something they are not, but taking advantage of every opportunity to lead, teach, and guide them through this world. Don't get me wrong, children are manipulated every day. If you are participating in this sort of thing, I encourage you to stop. If you are allowing it, as a father you must intervene on their behalf. One of the ways manipulation occurs is by not engaging your children on a personal level and allowing them to be influenced by things they don't fully understand. They always need an available father to discuss what they experience and feel. I am not telling you that you can raise perfect children, but you can guide them with every conversation you have. Respect your children enough to give them a fair shot at life. The objective is to allow them a better life than you had. When you show them what true respect is, you help them find how to treat others. Therefore, the golden rule is so important. Treat others the way you would want to be treated.

Chapter 4 | Forgiveness

What you're not promised is a perfect life. As a kid, you may have had a vision of what your life would become, and it is most likely miles away from what you considered or even expected. But there is hope. The most difficult thing to do on this journey we call life is to walk through it with the pain of unforgiveness. For each one of us, those effects of unforgiveness may be very different. The scars of parenting from a position of living in the past and the unhealthy methods or style you may have learned from your parents denies you the opportunity to find your true way. The loathing stench of a jaded worldview of people and life in general can lead you to parent from a place of bitterness that is debilitating to a child who has a natural inhibition to view the world and others in complete positivity. The paralyzing sting of being cold, indifferent, or hostile can cripple the ability of a child to express themselves, build healthy relationships, or find true self-worth. If your children see you with any one of those conditions, they will excuse it for a while, but eventually they become adults. And believe it or not, adults struggle with childhood trauma.

I just read recently that childhood trauma accounted for a two – three trillion-dollar cost for the US alone. The statistics were quite harsh. Suicide, self-harm, homicide, etc., were all categories to be greatly considered as byproducts. The therapy, medical, and prison reform costs were not directly mentioned, but I must believe they produce a second tier of even greater significance as a result from the primary cause. There obviously are more consequences to be considered and are surely unaccounted for. The larger gray area would be for the way in which children who come from abusive or hostile homes most likely end up pursuing coping methods that further harm them and never allow for complete healing. When a person stands alone and never feels accepted, the chances of them finding ways to express themselves harmfully grows expeditiously.

Scars

Normally, our wounds, if severe enough, require stitches. Sometimes injuries happen, and the proper treatment may not be available. There are alternative methods that can create the same scars but may not have been the proper way to handle a wound. No matter how tight you pull a bandage, no matter how much antibiotic cream you cram in, it's still not the proper treatment. At around ten years old, I was riding backwards and attempting to stand on a four-wheeler and fell off, landing on my back-shoulder blade. Thankfully a sharp rock stopped me from sliding across the ground and gashed my skin open and left me most definitely in need of stitches. I can say for certain; my family did not believe it did. Hence, the reason I know some families used the antibiotic and pull it tight method. You can spot this type of treatment based on the width of the scar left behind.

However, there is one part of the four-wheeler story I didn't include and that is the fact that my sister was driving. For years, I could not tell that story without blaming her for the accident.

Jokingly, of course, but as you know, truth sometimes exists there. I would blame her for the whiskey throttle that caused me to fall. But then later, as I matured, I realized it was never her fault. It was me. Had I not stood up, and turned backwards, it would have most likely never happened. I know it may be a minor injury or example to the thing that hurt you the most in your life. As a dad, you get to keep your scars for show and tell, but you don't get to pass on the pain of blame.

I am reminded of my father and how he has impacted my life in so many positive ways. However, his relationship with his father, on the contrary, was very unpleasant as it was full of drunken violence, discouraging words, intimidation's, and lack of affection. His father has now passed, but my dad has told me that his father only told him he loved him less than the five fingers on his one hand, over his entire life. But he never allowed that pain to stop him from being the father he believed he could be. And he became polar opposite to how his father verbally communicated love to him. I never once felt not loved by my father, because he has told me he loved me more times than all of the fingers, on all of the hands, of all of the people, I have met in my life. He made a conscious decision to not repeat what happened to him by word and deed and I am a better man for his effort and consistency. You have no excuses to pass pain along to your children and you have no right to roll the responsibility of fatherhood on anyone else because of the situation or circumstances you are in.

A father's great responsibility in his children's life is to protect them, not harm them. Perhaps you don't see it as an issue, because maybe nothing is "wrong" with you. And it may not be a matter of nothing being "wrong" with you at all. Perhaps it is best to consider your child first. We all have different life experiences and cannot jump to the conclusion that if it worked for me, it obviously would work for them as well. This way of thinking is the very culprit that breaks down and destroys the lines of communication we so desperately need. It is a complacent behavior and not seeking to improve the relationship.

As with our jobs, we can take on a strategy known as continuous improvement, which is an ongoing effort to improve products, services, and processes. These efforts can seek "incremental" improvement over time or "breakthrough" improvement all at once. So, in our relationships with our children, these can be inferred in the same way. We can easily define improvements first by the communications and interactions we have almost daily with our children. We can measure and analyze the opportunities against our own past, our resources, our unselfish expectations, and our willingness to listen to the voices of our children. I am not asking you to become a genie that grants every wish and most definitely not a door mat in any relationship. But instead, a father who is willing to offer correction and the opportunity to pursue happiness to your child. By doing so, you automatically take care of the last portion which is to guide, offer control, and help re-define the best path for their future. Parenting is never over; it just grows and develops into different stages of life. Most parents would agree that the major objective is to lead your children into a better place that allows them to build on what they were given, just like you hopefully did. Your children are not your enemy and do not deserve to be reminded of how you were treated as a child, but rather to be presented with the promise and accountability to reach a better future.

Stench

Never project a manipulated view of the world onto the innocence of a child's mind. Just because the cards you were dealt didn't play well at the table, it doesn't give you the right to let the hope out of a child's dreams. If you are leading your children into a place that only you feel safe, it's quite possible that you are doing it wrong. A child has the right to believe and pursue that which is written on their hearts. This is where we really develop the guidance and discovery portion of our fatherhood. They often imitate what they see in us, but also, we should seek to expand our boundaries for the sake of extending theirs. Stability is important, but how is that word defined? Are you looking for it to protect your child from something you never got over? Could it be that the incidents in your life have pushed you to a place of controlling everything to where you don't allow vision to be a part of your child's life? Often, vision or dreams are looked at as an uncontrollable risk to some people. When we choose to push our view of the world on our children, we can quench the drive for discovery and development that is naturally within them. You can probably think back to a time in your own life when you wanted to pursue something and were given a word of rejection sounding like this - "no". Don't get me wrong, no is okay, but not when delivered from a place of fear. We must lead our children from a place of trusting them as well. I often think of how a father could easily have suppressed this fire in the likes of a Mozart, Neil Armstrong, or Serena and Venus Williams. I think about the great visionaries who have worked for countless companies who decided to bring forth a zany idea that most of their colleagues may have laughed off, but someone believed in them.

Consider the everyday ordinary person who is deeply affected by the unbelief which is so common in the everyday life of people everywhere. "How dare you pursue something of importance or significance?", the naysayers quip. But to those who refuse ordinary, the extraordinary is possible. My eldest daughter always reminds me, it's not enough just to have dreams, you must also hold on to them, until they become reality. If your children can't discover their vision from your guidance, it makes it almost impossible for them to believe in themselves. They hunger and thrive naturally for your pride. Your belief in them is tied directly to the way in which you see the world. As a father, you can make the effort to not see your situation as what you don't have, but rather as a launch pad for their success. Sacrifice is a major theme in fatherhood, and the roles are endless in the film.

One thing most noticeable in a child is their ability for inspiration and invention. Sometimes not so much for adults. I'm reminded today of that as I look out at the snow. My four-year-old son and I were discussing the 8-10" of snow in our backyard and building a snow man. I told him it wasn't possible to build it because the snow was dry, and it couldn't be made into a ball. He had absolutely no problem responding with a solution. Within seconds, he responded, "But Dad, we can use tape." I burst out with laughter and it really created an unforgettable moment, but I learned something invaluable between the differences in the way we see life. It's a reminder to take a second look at the situation before opening my mouth. Maybe you can't make a snow man using tape, but how do you know? Have you ever tried? Maybe you just might learn something together and that's all that matters. So, get out there and give it a shot. Duct tape works for anything.

Sting

Customer service is the lifeblood of any business. There are certain companies that review systems have ultimately forced into better behavior and practices. And on the contrary, many others have closed because of them. If you have ever dealt with a company or paid for a service that was not to the standard you expected, you typically never forget it. If the reviews for a company say, "unfriendly staff" or "rude receptionist", normally that is enough to keep people from coming. Business is going to struggle if you get enough of those poor reviews. Children can forgive a bad mood or a little criticism here and there. But it is too much when it comes from a person whose role is to encourage and guide them. Just like that customer with the bad experience, they will eventually not return for service. A child is your greatest customer, but the currency required is far greater than gold or the almighty dollar. The words we use, our tone, and the expressions on our face are imprinted in the minds of our children. Children take the currency you give them at face value. Healthy communication involves hard work. We cannot just assume that because they are our children, they will listen better if we yell or that they will bend to our will if we use forceful words. Again, fear, intimidation, and threats are not signs of healthy parenting. Yes, of course, we all have our moments when we feel like nothing else will work, but we must focus on our long-term responsibilities and goals of parenting.

If you find yourself being overly critical of your child's mistakes or shortcomings, take a step back and think about the impact you are leaving on your future relationship. One day, this same child will be a parent and will learn the same methods of parenting from you. But that doesn't mean they will follow them to the tee, because we learn, we change, and we modify. Which is why I believe it is almost impossible to fulfill your role as a parent to the standards your children need if you are doing it from a place of criticality. Maybe it's the only place you know or understand, because it was the way you were taught. But, please consider the ways I outline in the book, and I don't think you will be able to deny the positive benefits and effects it will have on the relationships you so dearly value. The progression is one in which the thread of the story is maturity and the importance of helping not only your child find their best self, but you as well.

The way I have viewed forgiveness for many years is through a simple visual. I imagine the person who has offended me hanging onto the edge of a very high cliff by their fingertips. As I walk up to them in my mind, I ask the question - "Will I help them up or will I stomp on their fingers?" So far, I have never had a cliff hanger fall from the mountainside. Not saying I didn't step on one or two fingers, but not all of them. They've all survived, ok... That's all I'm saying. As a father, you typically don't go into it perfect or whole. Often, you have no idea what you just got yourself into. But one thing is certain, you're here now. When I reflect to times I have been hurt in my life, I can rarely think back to a time the other person said I'm sorry and I just magically got over it. In fact, many of the hurtful memories are available on demand instantly through a brain that seems to be hardwired to remind us of similarities from our past experiences. Most of the time it was because I came to a point of understanding or maturity that helped me to see the real resolve I had experienced was through an intentional commitment to move forward and choose to leave the pain behind. Just like the sun rises and sets upon the earth, people will attempt to hurt you.

People that are close to you will always be the most likely perpetrators to bring pain to your doorsteps. Your primary circle of influence knows your vulnerabilities and weaknesses greater than all of humanity itself and often will seem to thrive off the insecurities and lack of understanding you may have at times in this life. A very sadistic form of false sovereignty that is played out daily to help you know your place. These people can come in other forms than just your immediate family. They can be your coach, teacher, pastor, spouse, boss, friend, etc. Be aware that relationships with these people can influence and shape how you interact with your children. The scars that they have left behind are not always visible to the real world but show through with the finest of resolution to our children. They see through the mask and directly into your pain. If you don't think this is true, just ask them. That is truly a great place to start. Maybe they aren't old enough to see it, but just give it time. Perhaps, they are too old, so you might think, to have that conversation. Ask them anyways. Wouldn't you love to give that same feedback to your parents? Even more so if they are no longer around. Those people that we allow into the intimate portions of our lives have to be held to a standard for how they treat us and the way in which they interact with us. If you are parenting from a place of unforgiveness, chances are, the root cause is because someone mistreated you or caused you pain. However, this should never define how you treat those you love the most.

Three and a half years after becoming a father, I was divorced. It was not the vision I had for my life or my oldest daughter. As a five-year-old child, I experienced the long-lasting sting of what divorce can do to a family. I spent many nights crying for my parents to get back together and often questioned what I could have done differently to prevent it. It wasn't until many years later I understood that it was completely out of my control, as often is the case with childhood pain. It can take years to heal, and often it goes unchecked and spills over. And now, my own divorce was robbing me of the life I always vehemently claimed for myself and my future. It was robbing my daughter of the life I so desperately wanted for her.

And I would be lying if I didn't say that even sometimes as an adult, I drift away in thought and wonder what might have been if I would have been raised in a perfect home. Things may have been different, but I wouldn't be the father I am today had it not been that way. But isn't it easy to consider vain imaginations and not be focused on reality? Watch out, because you can do that with your parenting if you aren't careful. Time will slip away, and those children make the same mistakes, and the cycle just continues. All because no one decided to drive a stake in the ground and proclaim that this stops today. Many of these topics may be too fresh for you to instantly overcome, but if you remain diligent, time and prayer provide a way to work things out. I wrote a poem back then to remind me of the commitment I had for her –

The fussing and fighting have come to a cease,
one heart in devastation, the others at peace,
questions unanswered and life's rearranged.
My oh my, how things have changed.
She thinks and she wonders why things aren't the same;
is she to blame for all of this pain?
Mommy's not mommy, and dad's not dad,
her little life has become so sad,
she hides it with laughter, but inside she's mad.
Mad with dad, because he won't come home,
he's her new dad, "dad by phone".
A thousand explanations can't heal her frustrations,
but how can you fix this delicate situation?
Daddy's little girl, her heart in a whirl,
things will get better, just try not to let her,
run wild with imaginations or get caught in frustrations.
Time is the healer, now listen and feel her.
Being There – DB Smith

Parenting from a place of scars, stench, or sting never provides the guiding light a child needs in the darkness. When you are given responsibilities of fatherhood, it changes you. But that doesn't mean it makes all of our pain vanish. Yes, you can work through the pain, but not at the destruction of your family. As men, there are times we need to ask ourselves if the pain is interfering with the relationships that mean so much. And we can't just trust ourselves, we need the feedback and insight of those around us who love us and will be honest. It's called accountability. If you put off the important issues today and place your priorities in improper places in the name of coping, time will bring them back around. And the truth will show up at the most inconvenient time and in the shape of a pill most likely too painful to swallow. Like near the end of life, when we so often question the meaning and pursuits of the life we lived. I made the decision and declaration years ago that I have no intention to live a life focused on the things that may be a complete waste of time. No, I do not judge you if feel inspired to be a monk, professional hotdog eater, or if you want to climb a mountain. But if you are driven to those because you can't get healthy in your heart, don't be surprised later in life when truth knocks on the door; you were warned. Carrying that pain around with you damages your perception of reality and can cause you to chase wind and push you to forsake the ones you love.

Forgiveness is a requirement to live a healthy lifestyle. Stories of forgiveness have proven throughout history to be of the most powerful. The most rigid and hard individuals in life have crumbled under the weight of undeserving forgiveness. Especially those who have thought they could never receive it. Our memories seem to be hardwired to hold on to painful experiences and it feels almost impossible to move on at times. But no matter what your parents, or the world, or even yourself has done to you, it is possible to forgive and move on. If you show me a parent who gives a valiant effort to live a life full of forgiveness, I will show you someone with valiant children. They will live by the example they see and will always seek to find the best in a world that may be imperfect, but full of hope, nonetheless.

In prior speaking engagements, I have challenged people in the audience to find a partner and stand directly in front of them at arm's length and do the following five things. I call it the *"five-step recovery"*. I swear it's not awkward, especially when it is with someone who needs to be reminded of this simple message.

- *Look one another deeply in the eyes for 10-15 seconds*
- *Exchange the words "I don't love you" and return to the gaze*
- *Experience the moment and repeat with the phrase "I love you"*
- *Return to the gaze, and experience the real shift in your soul*
- *Hug it out and don't forget to smile*

What cannot be ignored is the powerful shift and impact in the room. I have seen entire rooms of people deeply affected by such a simple exercise in communication. It is a spectacle to witness the power of our words and to know that another person can express so much in so few words. TO be loved is life, TO not be loved is death. People have later expressed to me that the experience helped them to put their life and relationships back in the right context and to see themselves more clearly in the eyes of the person they so deeply love. Communication had broken down because of not saying what needed to be said. But saying the things that were the bookend extremes in the simplest ways radically changed the condition of the relationship. That is what I call a breakthrough and it only took one minute to get there. Remember that in the laws of continuous improvement, change can be made in both ways, incrementally or in a complete breakthrough. You must decide what the relationship between you and your children needs. The spirit of the words you speak are as important as the actions and views you share with them. Forgiveness has the power to end wars in reality, but also in the battlefield of the heart and mind. Take a moment and ask for help weighing out the condition of the relationships you value. Always try to be the initiator, after all it is your job to lead by example.

Chapter 5 | Commitment

When I visualize commitment, I see our brave and noble service men and women of the military who give everything for the greater purpose of protecting our freedom. And from there it grows to the higher levels of organizational hierarchy and their commitment to show they are willing to support, maintain, change, or improve any situation together. In the domestic case of our branches of government or international groups like NATO. It doesn't always mean it can be for the good of another entity or organization. In the case of war for example. Many soldiers have fallen or must have at least felt that it was an imminent fate at times of war when they lost communication or didn't have proper guidance from the command centers they were working with. Parenting is the same way. With your commitment you are offering direction at a higher level to your child. And the reception of that direction is received when they trust our commitment to them.

From early on, children trust us, but then they begin to look to us for direction. This is how they learn to navigate the world. Remember that commitment is the arena where trust, respect, and forgiveness operate. Your dedication to your children must be proven in that arena. As children age, they learn to question everything, and many times over you will need to prove you are on their side. Whether it's spoken out loud or not. Commitment can be viewed as an undying loyalty, but I believe it is even more dynamic. In this chapter we will look at different aspects of commitment and how critical they are for any relationship, especially with our children.

Self-sacrifice

Young Anne Sullivan had no idea what she had gotten herself into when she met the six-year-old Helen Keller. Helen was deaf, blind, and could not speak because of bouts with fever and sickness she suffered as an infant. Conditions that would frustrate Helen into uncontrollable rage. When Helen's parents were fraught with desperation, they decided to bring in a twenty-year-old from Massachusetts; Anne Sullivan. Anne had empathy for Helen regarding her own personal issues with poor vision and considered this to be a challenge she was willing to accept. Helen would prove to make that decision very difficult for her, often physically assaulting her and completely ignoring her. The Keller's knew Anne was their daughters only hope. Anne never gave up on her and even developed a new method of teaching for Helen's condition, known as "touch teaching". Touch teaching is when you allow the person of disability to place their hand in yours and spell out what they are trying to communicate through sign language all while you are interpreting their signs by physical touch. That is incredibly clever was revolutionary thinking. I don't think Anne Sullivan ever received enough credit for her brilliance. Anne stayed by Helen's side for almost fifty years, until she passed at the age of seventy. Throughout their friendship, Anne also taught Helen to read, write, and speak. Can you imagine what that must have been like? To be a twenty-year-old and dedicate your life to the servitude of this little girl? This would have been quite a daunting challenge for anyone.

I am sure Helen was also afraid of the world. She was almost in a state of ferality, having never been around other people or even able to communicate. And in sharp contrast, we feel overwhelmed at times when our children are slightly misbehaving. Quite humbling in retrospect, if you ask me. I believe Anne Sullivan was a saint. She willingly gave of herself and offered her full dedication to someone who severely needed her. The Keller's would surely be able to tell the greatest firsthand account of what they saw unfold in the life of their child. The Keller's are not alone in the fact that they are the only ones to have children with disabilities. It is especially painful to know that some children are given over to institutions because of these difficulties. However, there are parents who I admire and feel underqualified in their company because of their complete ability to love and provide for these children.

We have had several friends with children that have Down syndrome, and I have observed the patience and overwhelming love firsthand. Some of the greatest children I have come in contact with have what society would consider disabilities, but I consider them to possess superpowers. Their ability to be genuine and sincere in everything they say and do is quite pure and inspiring. Their true difference is not their perceived disabilities, but it is seen in their special attributes and the very special people they have as a support system that help them along the way and cause all of us to have a new perspective on the possibilities of life.

Maybe your child feels alone now. It is worth finding out, if you don't know. Your child needs you to stand with them no matter what comes their way. Your child needs you to put their needs ahead of yours. They should know that they have your love and devotion, no matter whether you fully agree with their decisions or not. You don't get to disown or disavow your children, no matter what you've seen or heard. They are given one father who will wade out in the deep waters of life to rescue them, even if they made the mistake of going out there. When your children know you are committed to them, they will commit to you. And as they grow old, that commitment will strengthen.

If you think fear will hold them, you are wrong. Creating fear in your child may work for now, but rest assured, it will push them away. Yes, they respect you, but when they fear you, they will resist or crumble under your pressure for only so long. The objective of true commitment is to have them desire you because they know you would do anything for them, even lay down your own life. Fear eventually pushes your child further away from you. Threatening intimidation forces your child to question whether you are for them or against them. I can imagine that Anne Sullivan had moments of frustration, but she never operated with tactics outside the boundaries of true love and servitude.

Be committed to use patience, understanding, and guidance as your tools. But most of all, you will need to set yourself and your personal interests aside at times to convey your love. Your job has never called you to come home. Promotions come and go, opportunities knock, and bosses growl, but you only get so few chances to do what really matters. Sometimes life has a way of throwing you headlong into situations we never planned for or even expected. So, while you have the chance, make the adjustments now to do the right thing. Make sure your priorities are in order while you are chasing your titles, jockeying for positions, and climbing that corporate ladder. Just don't let the rat race be the only thing you're willing to sacrifice for.

Protection

I know Jesus was the first to make the statement, "No greater love has any man than to lay down his life for his friend." But I personally know of a time this was displayed in real life. Back home there are two wooden crosses by a famous NASCAR facility. Very unassuming as they sit right off the side of the road in front of a large open field. But what transpired there tells this story of what Jesus meant in full blown reality. When these races are scheduled, hundreds of thousands of people make plans to attend and camp out at the campgrounds near the race. Often, they stay there for one week, sometimes longer. It is a time for friends to get together and catch up on old times and a time to make new memories. People come from everywhere for the total experience that is much more than for the races. It should be quite the celebration… However, those crosses represent something tragic amongst good times shared. These two crosses are for the two men who died on race week at their campsite. These two guys were best friends and had been here several times together through the years. They both knew their responsibilities at camp when they arrived and started immediately. One of them grabbed the metal flagpole and prepared it to put up their favorite drivers' race flag high above the campsite. He assembled the pole on the ground until it was almost twenty feet in length, dug a hole, and then planned to erect it in front of the camper. He failed to notice the power line directly above the campsite as he erected it. As he hit the power line with the flagpole, instantly he was electrocuted. His friend seeing this, panicked and did the only thing he had in his heart. He ran at him and tried to knock him away from the pole. He was also killed instantly. Oh, what a tragedy. This was never the intention of the trip and it was never expected. But this friend laid down his life for his friend and this was love demonstrated. I think about these two gentlemen every time I see those old wooden crosses when I return home. May we demonstrate that same heart and willingness to protect our children's lives whenever necessary. You may be feeling judgmental or overly critical about the story, but I believe that is the way protection works within the boundaries of commitment to our loved ones. Taking a bullet for someone is outside of the boundaries, but doing it for your children, it is immediately back in. Don't forget that. Love doesn't always count the cost but propels you to battle even if you carry not a weapon. The way we view protecting our children does not always include complete situational evaluation.

We must be the voice of protection they need. Yes, they need to stand up for themselves and oppose people who push adversity in their face. But we are the responsible parties who oversee and guide them. I don't advocate fighting little kids on the playground, so don't think about it. But don't fail them when they need you. Throw caution to the wind when your child is in danger or in desperation. There are very few times that a child can feel threatened and how we protect them teaches them about our true commitment. They should never question your willingness to defend them. It doesn't give them a pass to do whatever they want. They will still need correction from time to time. After all, part of your job is to give them the correction they need, not just discipline.

Display protection every chance you get to help build the security they need. You are the hand to hold. You are the warm blanket in the cold for your child. You are the flashlight on the dark road. You are the gas delivered when the car is out of it on the side of the road. You are the car that picks them up at a party they need to leave. You are the words in their ears when they can't hear. You are the eyes when they can't see. You eliminate the fear and shadows from their life. You are their father.

Endearment

You set the standard for how your children are treated and what they are willing to accept when considering commitment to another individual. I don't play around when it comes to my daughters and who they intend to marry one day. Those matters are of the utmost importance to me. I cannot control the decisions they make, but I have every intention to influence them to the best of my ability.

Years ago, I decided to dedicate time to take my daughters out on individual dates and treat them how I expect their potential significant other to treat them when they were older. These dates started while all three of my oldest were still very young. I only refer to them during the date with endearing names or as "my date". So, for example, I might say something like, "How was dinner my love, and would my date like to go somewhere after dinner?" I made sure to pull out the chairs for them, open doors, take their jackets, etc. Whatever it took to make them know that I admired them. Isn't that what every father wants for his children to find in a spouse one day. I often get requests for daddy date nights and depending on my answer, there are intense arguments that ensue because it may or may not be one of their turns. My intention is to have them understand what it means to be treated with dignity and adoration. I don't put myself in the position to make them feel awkward or weird. I keep it in the context of courting. I know that may be an old school term when it comes to relationships, but still very applicable.

The dates taught me that they began to set their own standards of what they are willing to accept as well. They have a place of reference now in their mind to compare what they want and what they don't. They will be much more unwilling to accept any behavior that is disrespectful or not well thought out. They know what they want, and they can more easily pursue it with full confidence. If you don't think it matters, you are sadly mistaken. Many of the people tied to bad spousal relationships today could have greatly benefited from having a father who could help them from accepting something not worthy of their love. All the warning signs are always there. Yes, people change, but why start a relationship out based on things that won't last and especially when you can identify that someone is not truly endearing to you early on. If the objective is to fall in love, why would you settle for a sub-par standard. I am not raising princesses, but I am raising them to use their ears, mind, and hearts. They realize they are not perfect and by seeing their imperfections, it causes them to be more accepting and see others more truthfully. I cannot guarantee this is the perfect advice, but it is exceedingly better than doing nothing at all.

I have a four-year-old son now and we haven't started daddy dates yet, but I can't wait. I plan to teach him what it means to be a gentleman and how to be courteous and pay attention to the one he plans to show his affection. I want him to also be a good listener and considerate of others. I don't want to miss opportunities to teach him how. I want to give him everything I have, because I love him. I never want my children to not feel like I didn't give them my all. Because that is what fathers do.

I once had a close friend whose mother had a stroke. It left her completely debilitated. Not able to speak or move. His father left her. He couldn't deal with the situation and thought it would be better if he just restarted his life. He left her and everything behind him. His son hated him for abandoning their family and his mother. His mother eventually regained her speech and learned how to walk again. His father was there for none of this. It was heartbreaking to see it all play out this way. It hurts to know that someone could leave the one they love in a time that they need them most. My friend sadly still doesn't speak with his father and has become the main caregiver in the family to his mother. He couldn't marry because he lost all value in the idea and because he had dedicated all his energy to taking care of his mother. He has told me she was the only woman he ever loved. Even more reason, actions are louder than words. Empty commitment is based on passing emotions rather than unwavering allegiance. Wedding vows are important. They contain a base line for the type of commitment you are partaking in. Have a look -

I, _____, take you, _____, to be my wife/husband, to have and to hold from this day forward, for better, for worse, for richer, for poorer, in sickness and in health, to love and to cherish, until we are parted by death. This is my solemn vow."

As I read that, I am dually reminded of the unspoken commitment we have with our children to do the same thing. You must do everything in your power to take care of them, nurture their unique qualities, and help them find their way. Your actions will ultimately prove what you believe.

Investment

Taking the time and effort necessary to earn and show your commitment is an investment. That's what makes it all the greater. The investment is when we discover the long-term process of commitment. An investment is when you expect greater returns that exceed your original contribution. For fun I like to read old investment books that stake claims to riches if you invest in the stock market and other modes of creating wealth. Normally what they predict is far from what played out, because of a multitude of factors but, nonetheless. I respect financial investments and see them as highly valuable, but there are no get rich quick schemes for most people in this lifetime. I think by now we should realize that. Be responsible, yes, be uninformed, no. Many fathers expect one or two talks to complete the work necessary, but that is not how this works. It is the process of investing consistently and with true conviction that matters. Slow and steady wins the race.

Years ago, I remember hearing the worth of retired General David Petraeus, in terms of investment, and it was in the millions. And the government didn't just invest money in him, but also years of commitment for the development of his leadership. One day, a scandal broke that he had been unfaithful to his wife and in doing so, he shared unclassified information. Keep in mind that this man wrote internal military training programs, developed the Army's doctrinal manuals, trained the Army's officers, and supervised the Army's center for the collection and distribution of official war documentation. This man was an icon of nobility and would have never been expected to behave in this way. This investment was now considered a waste by many when the news hit the press. To boot, he was also considered to be the greatest General of our time, as he was widely known and prestigiously decorated. However now he was being forced into retirement and possibly facing criminal charges. Now, no longer able to serve as General, his own personal investments had faltered under the weight of his failure. So, in your situation, maybe you have made mistakes with your children, where they expected a higher standard from you, and you pulled a Petraeus. You let them down in a major way. There is still hope. Like I said earlier, the government could have been much worse on him but showed mercy. Children are much more merciful than the government or at least I would hope so. If you feel that the relationship has faltered because you squandered the investments you made or maybe you never made any in the first place, I want to help you make the effort to change. You must renew your commitment with your children, while there is time. When you run out of time, it is much harder to communicate what needs to be said.

When you sow in the now and in the future of your children, you will reap for yourself a great harvest one day. Be the example of what it looks like to be invested in them. I cannot say it enough, actions speak louder than words. When you come home early to take them out for dinner or when you show up to a school event and surprise them, they see you in a different light. One that causes them to believe you are committed to the relationship. Our brains are powerfully creative and can come up with fantastic ideas that will blow the socks off our children. I don't offer a calendar with the book for you to schedule with, but if your heart is in the right place and you let them know they are important to you, you will take care of business.

When I was a kid, I remember my dad working in his shop, and I would go out and beg him to stop and play ball with me. Although sometimes I had to beg extra hard, he never let me down. We would get out there with my family and setup a couple of ragtag bases and use a whiffle ball and bat and play a game of backyard baseball. It was quite often that we did this. It helped me to realize at an early age that my father was committed to me and properly invested in me. He could have easily stayed focused on whatever he was piddling with in his shop, but he knew what was important. As a result, I didn't become a Major League Baseball player, but I learned the value of someone giving you their time. And that is what it really comes down to when I talk about investment.

As your most valuable commodity, time is the most important dynamic of commitment. It may cost you money if it is because you are losing overtime at work, but you are the one who must count that cost. I know we must provide for our families, and we must do what it takes to pay the bills. But we can't fall victim to the cycle that breaks down families everyday across America and many other places across the world. Like it or not, you are not here to work only. You are here to invest in the lives of others and enrich their experience. The same way in which others have done for you. Look back and be grateful for the people who invested in you and saw your potential and drew it out. Now pay it forward. We may fail and we may falter, but if we stay committed to that which was entrusted to us, we will prevail. Our children will bloom into something magnificent. And because of that, when you grow old, you will never have to worry about not having them there by your side. And that sounds like a solid investment to me.

Chapter 6 | A father's role

Our culture is inundated with entertainment. Whether it be movies, theme parks, sports, music, games, or videos, we are all but bored. However, in the words of the great English poet, Alexander Pope, "amusement is happiness for those who cannot think." If anyone was qualified to talk about amusement, he could, because he was only 54" tall. And as you know that is the magic number for access to all amusement park rides. Oh, the irony. But, could his statement be true? And what does it mean to be amused? The term amuses or amusement appeared in France in the 1640's. It meant "to create a diversion of attention." Before that it was used in the Greek as "bemuse", which meant "to be without muses or teachers" or "to be uneducated." Obviously, Pope was on to something. You will resolve issues with your children by taking them to amusement parks in the same way as if you buy your significant other a gift as a peace treaty to excuse infidelity. Entertaining distraction is the only true form of entertainment taking place. You can't buy anyone's love. You can't take them places and expect the relationship to automatically improve. Have fun, yes. Misuse amusement for your children, no.

In our family, years ago, my wife and I decided to be very intentional about the entertainment we would allow for our children. We studied certain "family friendly" tv shows they were watching and noticed that most of the time, there wasn't a father figure or if there was, he was portrayed as a doofus. If we found that the father was made out to be absent minded or not displayed with dignity, we would cancel the show in our home. One of the most common themes in those types of shows were the disregard of influence and the lack of respect we saw towards the father role. I have read estimations of 20-30 million children in the US don't have a father in the home and that half of that number is considered to have not seen their father in the last year. Sounds like a bit of an epidemic to me. So, amid an epidemic, the role of a father must be upheld to standards that promote the stability of a complete family. I must believe fatherlessness is the main culprit for why networks have moved away from displaying fathers in the correct manner.

Let's look at a brief synopsis through a tv timeline of the role of a father. Andy Griffith portrayed a loving father who was willing to offer guidance and correction. He would even take time to openly speak with Opie about life in general and take time to teach him whenever he would personally make mistakes. Mike Brady, of "The Brady Bunch", intentionally taught his children in a loving way and was a great encourager. Cosby was also one of the great tv fathers. He loved and taught his children that they had a very valuable place in this world. Al Bundy, from "Married with Children", was one of the first father roles I remember that really started to approach fatherhood from a very negative angle. Whatever he did and said often came from a place of disdain for his children and it showed. Most of what he did was a punchline to signal the fake audience laughter that would negatively influence the real significance of being a father. Carl Winslow, of "Family Matters", had times where he could be a father, but for the most part only interjected one liners and lacked true substance. Danny Tanner, of "Full House", was interesting because he was accompanied by two other characters of influence; "Uncle Joey and Uncle Jesse." One playing a dimwit for the majority and the other as the role of anything goes. However, Danny played a father very well. His engagement and ability to interact with his daughters was one of the best in my memories. He was always in the mode of self-sacrifice and providing the best environment for his children. Tim "The Tool Man" Taylor, did a fantastic job with humor and masculinity and tried to give some thought to the communication with his sons. All these men played a role in a generation of children to see different social dynamics at work in the lives of many families.

So, considering my brief personal summary, where do you see yourself along the tv spectrum of parenting? Are you obnoxious or caring or blighted or just overbearing? Maybe it's your children who should give you the news here. Of course, none of us are perfect tv fathers. But, when you consider the generation of father's that were portrayed for children years ago, they were far better than the absence of father roles shown thereafter to children of today. Through conversations with my children, they were not able to think of any shows containing a strong fatherly influence. So, for all the children in fatherless homes, the chances of determining what a father is can be quite slim. The best hope for them is that they have a grandpa, stepdad, foster parent, coach, or uncle who would be able to show them positive male attributes and fatherly love and guidance. Sometimes, I know that isn't the case, and very strong mother's step up and step into that role. I believe some women do extraordinary things in the lives of their children with the adversity that comes when fathers abandon their children. My grandmother was one of those extraordinary women forced into the role of both father and mother when my alcoholic grandfather decided to abandon his role. In the 1960's, she raised four children by herself, worked full time, and paid her house off. What a powerful testimony of a mother who sacrificed everything for her children. Meanwhile, my now late grandfather rambled and slowly committed his life to destroying his relationships with his children. Thankfully, towards the end of his life, he recovered from alcoholism and ran local AA meetings, but never fully recovered from the damage caused by the abandonment.

Every day you make the decision about what kind of father you are going to be. If you want to take the role of a good and present father, you've got to be there and work hard at it. I recently watched a Ted Talk by Marshall Davis-Jones titled "Spell Father." He started the spoken word story by talking about being in the final round of the spelling bee as a child and he was asked to spell father. He spelled father as "m-o-t-h-e-r." Then he went on to explain the fact that his father had abandoned him, and his mother assumed the fatherly role. It was very touching and represented the life for many children today. I value and respect the women who are the only parent their children know. Chances are, that as you are reading this book, you may be a byproduct of a fatherless home. I don't have to write much down for you to know firsthand exactly what that was like. Maybe you didn't have a father at home, but maybe you had your mom, your grandfather, an uncle, stepfather, or even a brother who stepped into that role. Be thankful for that. If you are a father who has failed, set your failures aside and focus on rebuilding. And now let's look at a few aspects I would like you to consider in the role of a father.

Guidance

Have you ever been alone and lost in the woods? It can be terrifying, especially in the dark. Why? It's the culmination of one of our greatest fears as human beings. Scientists refer to it as the fear that rules them all or the root of all fears. Xenophobia. Which is the fear of the unknown. Most of us have it to some degree. I was recently in the mountains with my son and it was getting dark. For fun, I decided to teach him how to howl. Where we were is known for having coyotes, but don't worry, we were safe. As we started howling together, we started creating the perfect pitch you need to spark the coyotes howl. Then we remained quiet and tuned our ears into the distance. And at last, we heard a faint howl in the dark. Immediately, I realized my son heard it too as I felt him climbing up my body hurriedly for safety from the noise. I couldn't believe how quickly he scurried up. It was quite the effort. He was very afraid, even trembling. It was all fun and games until he heard the howl. But isn't that exactly the way life is? We start out doing something we don't quite understand and then suddenly, something happens that can scare you nearly to death. In those moments of not knowing what in the world is going on, wouldn't you prefer someone there to guide you through it. Well, the good news is, that's your job as a father. You are to be the guide to your children. I didn't say boss them around aimlessly. No, guide them. No matter how young or old your children are, you can help guide them. I was my son's guide in that moment of holding him when he was afraid. And in the moment of helping him to see that he was protected.

Too many people think guiding someone means to bark out orders or micromanage every decision someone makes. That's not at all what I mean by guidance. Guidance is love accompanied with the effort of giving them the tools to be successful in any situation. Lewis and Clark had passion and compasses to navigate the American wilderness. Vikings had fearless ambition and sun stones to navigate cloudy skies across treacherous seas. And you have an appetite succumbed to hunger and your GPS to navigate the concrete jungles to find your local fast food joint. Things have definitely changed when it comes to our nature for adventure and ability to navigate. However, we all use what's in our heart and the tools we've been given to navigate life. Right or wrong, we have all had certain tools or skills handed down to us. What tools are you handing down to your children? How about some of these? The ability to read, managing time, how to treat others, how to speak, to value truth, managing money, and taking responsibility.

When the Boy Scouts Association was founded in England in 1908 by Sir Baden-Powell, he created the Scout motto "Be Prepared." It was later adopted by the Boy Scouts of America as well. However, Baden-Powell, an English soldier, stated that the reason behind the motto was so that young men could always be in a state of readiness of mind and body to do your duty. That very principle has been the guiding light to millions of children. The pragmatic understanding of being prepared has so many layers of meaning that can be applied to any situation. It positions someone to always look for ways to help or do or engage. That idea is the fundamental thought behind guiding your children. You are making them alert to the world and the interactions that can take place. Obviously, you cannot plan for everything because there will always be an element of surprise. For example, you are sending your children off to school and you know how school can be for any child. When they get to school, they will not have you there to physically guide them from class to class, and frankly they may not want you to. However, you should at least be in their mind. Your guidance will lead them to make right choices and always consider whatever good or bad offers they may receive at school. Strong communication and meaningful conversations may help them to not feel insecure if someone makes a crude comment or makes them feel uncomfortable. And, also noteworthy because we are living in an epidemic of teen suicide now. Many times, it stems from in school or online bullying and then the child often makes the decision to take their life. They need the ability to navigate and learn ways to properly deal with any situation head on. Two are always stronger than one. When your child knows they have you helping them along the way, they will more likely be open to discuss even the toughest of topics.

Stability

A Congressional Medal of Honor, a Nobel Laureate, a civil rights movement, a complete cultural shift, and a collection of museums displaying countless mementos all rest upon an initial act of bravery by a 15-year-old girl who was given the gift of stability. Claudette Colvin was a young lady who sparked the civil rights movement in Montgomery, Alabama on March 2, 1955. She has not received the recognition she deserved and often, people may not even recognize the name. Jim Crowe law's prevented African Americans from sitting in the front of the public transportation buses in the presence of whites. If they were seated, they were to give up their seats and move to the back of the bus, no matter what age or gender. One day, young Ms. Colvin refused. The three other women seated with and across the aisle from her got up and moved to the back, but she remained seated. I listened to an interview of her as she had progressed in years and she noted that as she was told to give up her seat, "history held her firmly in that seat". She said it was as if Harriet Tubman and Sojourner Truth had placed their hands upon her shoulders and pushed her back down. The bus driver had the authority to remove her from her seat and the bus. When she did not heed the instructions to move, the police were called, and they physically removed her and took her to the county jail. Her parents heard the report from their daughter and immediately called a lawyer. The case was eventually brought before the Alabama Supreme Court and years later was ruled in her favor. Her initial act of bravery would spark so many other bus sit ins and even nine months later the very famous Rosa Parks to act in the same way. Rosa Parks later received the Congressional Medal of Honor. During this time, Dr. Martin Luther King Jr. had begun speaking out in peaceful protests and rallies across the country. And for his work, receiving the Nobel Peace prize. Her tiny wave crashing on the shores was now gaining full momentum to become a massive tsunami from an ocean of people who had grown tired of being oppressed.

It saddened my heart to read her stories and accounts of growing up as a black child in the South. There were many horrific things done to people of color in the name of good and in the name of God. Claudette told the story of shopping for shoes and I realized there is still so much many of us don't understand or can't properly relate to. Being allowed to enter a place of business was not permitted through the front door so the only possible chance of service was to go to the back side of the store. And the only way to get new shoes from the department store, if you weren't turned away, was to trace the shape of your foot on a brown paper bag and then give it to the clerk and hope they gave you the right size. There were separate restrooms and separate water fountains for people of color.. The shame and the pain were real. But in all this pain, great changes came because of one special little girl. I believe it all stemmed from one often overlooked gift we receive from great parents.

Claudette Colvin was adopted at the age of four, by her parents C.P. and Mary Colvin. I can only imagine what might have happened to her if she didn't have her parents to give her stability. It is the most basic parental provision we so often overlook and underappreciate. In turmoil, it is almost impossible for a child to find their voice or even be brave. I truly believe the home in which she was raised empowered her to see the world in a different light. I believe she was grounded in a strong home and by strong parents. I think it is evidenced even further by the fact that her parents were willing to get a lawyer and fight until justice was served. Imagine the times they lived in and how brave you would have to be to pursue legal action against people that could have easily killed or lynched you and your family.

When we provide a stable home for our children, they learn they have our support and we are fostering their ability to think for themselves and help develop a proper value system that gives them the opportunity to build foundational principles to live by. Right now, across America, there are children who do not have an environment conducive to form a proper home education or ideology of life. I don't have a pie chart to show you or statistics to share from life across America, but I can assure you we have all heard or experienced the stories of what life is like for children in bad home situations. My children have had plenty of their school mates confide in them the terror they endure by a raging father or nights of not having food. In some cases, you can help, but not all. If you sense a child could be in danger it is important to contact authorities. If you read or watch the news you can easily see the neglect of some parents out there. Abusive parenting destroys stability in the mind of a child. It must stop if you are physically or mentally abusive to your children. A child needs to know that their father is consistent, reliable, and trustworthy. If you make a promise, do everything you can to keep it. Your future depends on it.

The other major problem facing children today regarding stability is the absence of the father in the home, as pointed out earlier. Fathers can make choices that can keep them from the home, some can be selfish, and some can be criminal. Many fathers are trying to be fathers from prison. I understand that people can make mistakes that have enforceable consequences, but it does not allow you to opt out from parenting. When I weigh out what it means to be a father, I can't imagine allowing anything coming between my children and me. Not even prison bars. If you value something, you always put forth the effort to prove it. The nature of most men is to be highly competitive. Often to the point of complete sacrifice of our bodies. We can pursue sports and endure all levels of pain and injuries all in the name of victory. I can assure you if you put that same effort and commitment into being a father, no matter what state of being you are in, you will achieve an even greater victory, in life. So, whatever stability looks like for you, I don't know. But whatever it is, be sure to offer the best platform for your children to know that someone out there believes in them and will never abandon them.

Elevation

Passion is quite a complicated topic and can be very difficult to ascertain for most. Some people know from birth what type of occupation or hobby they are interested in pursuing with their life. I have met people who could play the guitar from age five and I have met people who knew they wanted to become a doctor early on and unwaveringly became one later in life. I find these types of people quite incredible. But are they or is there a secret? Obviously, certain people are created with certain giftings that seem to be from another world. However, just as stability gives the platform, elevation offers the nurturing development that children need to reinforce and understand their strengths and abilities. It also allows you the ability to be honest with yourself and your motives for your children. Don't be disappointed if your children don't want to follow in your footsteps or even share the same dreams you do. If you realize that you can sometimes get in the way of the development of a child's strengths and abilities, you have overcome half of the battle. Determination, commitment, and focus are the other half. You cannot force your child to be something they are not.

A prime example is Todd Marinovich, a short-lived former quarterback in the NFL for the Los Angeles Raiders. ESPN put out a documentary in 2011 titled "The Marinovich Project." Marv Marinovich was the first NFL strength and training coach for the Oakland Raiders. His incredible hunger to be the best in this newly established field was insatiable. Strength and training coaches are responsible for developing players to perform at their greatest potential; kind of like what I am describing in a father for this section. It is quite impressive that he basically started something which is a major staple for the success of many athletic programs today. And remember, these are elite athletes in the NFL. Most of them already at the top of their game. However, Marv was an expert in getting the most out of his players. When Todd was young, his father made him perform routines and drills endlessly. He pushed his son to become the best he could be. It was a perfect scenario to place a malleable child in the hands of a father who loved him dearly and was a complete expert in athletic development; or was it? Todd went on to break California high school passing records and be drafted to the NFL. But that career would last less than three years. In that span, he became addicted to drugs and was booted from the NFL. How could this even be possible? His father put everything he had into making him a great quarterback. They referred to Todd in high school as "Robo QB". But I think the facts of the matter can be established from a statement Todd made in the documentary. He said, "Just because you are good at something, doesn't mean you're born to do it." Cold hard facts. Marv would have probably fared better to have allowed his son to develop a love for the game. There is a fine line in forcing your child to find their strengths and abilities. A father can kill the love of something, or he can find ways to keep the fire burning.

Michael Jordan told Ahmad Rashad in an interview years ago that "the greatest thing about basketball was his love and passion for it". "And the love he had for it drove him to the extreme to maintain that love". "And to be the best at anything, you've got to have love for it". All of this stemmed from the question "what has basketball taught you?" The first thing I noticed is there was absolutely no technical jargon or explanations about discipline or even about being the best. Nope. It was his love for the game itself that drove him into the pursuit to maintain the love. He himself could never be satisfied with anything else. I think this is the glaring difference in the two stories.

Imagine Michael Jordan being trained in the same way, with a father who revolutionized a professional sport. Imagine the pressure, strain, and limitations that could have been put on him. Or maybe he could have been even better, but that is not what my gut tells me. Your love as a father should never overwhelm a child's passion for doing something. I fully understand every child is not exceptional at everything they pursue and that we live in a world where we glorify winning. But in the case of our children, it is not about winning or losing, or failure and victory, or even being the best at something. What it is truly about is helping your child to find that same love for something, just as Michael Jordan spoke about, and elevate them to find their own definition of greatness. Remember that when your child doesn't perform the way you think they should.

Promotion

If you are so fortunate to help your child find their talents, strengths, or abilities, it is no longer enough to just coach them along within the parameters of yourself. One of the greatest things a father can do is help their children find their own way. I love hearing stories of great CEO's who make statements about hiring people smarter than you. Mark Cuban, Steve Jobs, Jeff Bezos; all billionaires who share this belief. Could you for one moment consider that your children may be smarter than you? Maybe you should. The sooner a child learns to believe in themselves, the sooner they develop into something amazing. The belief you give your children can propel them into a mindset of taking risks, eliminating fears, and exploring the great unknowns. We must work to eliminate the limitations we put over our children and expectations that hold them back from being the absolute best versions of themselves. I love joking with my children that they receive great attributes from me, but I never miss the opportunity to promote them individually in light of their own wonderful characteristics. It is hard enough out there for people to find true acceptance and be appreciated for who they are individually. As a father, I never want my children to be driven by my expectations to the point of failure.

Just the opposite, I want them to attain the goals they set, together, and allow them to feel the success that comes along with it. I want to give them the push it takes to remain focused and not give up. I want them to finish what they start, learn the lessons, make the decisions, be bold, and keep on keeping on. A father can be the greatest motivator in a child's life.

When my oldest daughter was around ten years old, I was running a 5k almost every weekend. She approached me with the idea of running the next race with me. I told her it wasn't that easy. I told her we would need to start training together and set a goal to run a race several weeks out. She agreed and we began to train. It wasn't as easy as she expected. In fact, she considered quitting after the first week. I wouldn't let her. We had committed to something and we were not going to stop because of a little discomfort. During the training, it gave me opportunities to identify her struggles and help her find ways to overcome what she was feeling. Because, as you may know, running for the most part is mental. Yes, you can condition the body, but the mind sometimes is willing to put up quite the fight. When I first started running longer distances years ago, a very close friend of mine always advised me to do a mental check when I wanted to quit. Are your legs ok? Are your arms ok? Do you have any pain? How are your lungs? How are your feet? Ninety nine percent of the time, it was my brain telling me to stop without any ailments. Funny how that works. I helped her to use the same check-up method I had learned from my friend. And the other method I learned on my own was to always focus my mind on one word. One word. Persevere. I explained to her that when I felt as though I was running out of gas, I needed to fight back against my brain and the way I would do it was by repeating my word. She didn't know what that word meant at the time, but she would soon find out firsthand. We trained for probably five or six weeks and then we signed up and ran our first 5k together. She told me her own personal goal was to not stop running the entire time. I encouraged her that this would be a real challenge, but I commended her for her goal and respected that she was thinking about the experience. She wanted to make the most out of it and I am sure wanted to prove to me that she could do it.

The race started and we set off to a good pace. Soon we had our first two miles in the books, and now we were on to our third. She looked to be a little fatigued with her red cheeks and falling ponytail. I would occasionally ask her how she felt, and she would nod or give me a thumbs up. And if you know anything about running, this is normally where you are at almost full exertion. You begin to lose the ability to want to talk in order to conserve energy for the final stretch. All runners know that you never want to finish a race with gas left in the tank. With the finish line less than half a mile away, I saw her switch into another gear and the expression on her face changed. There was a renewed focus in her eyes. We began to pick up the pace. Within two tenths of a mile she was almost sprinting to the finish line. And it was quite the site to see! I was quite impressed that she finished so strong! I went to grab a water for her after we crossed and when I got back to her she proclaimed, "I did it!" I will never forget that moment. She had made a statement that meant so much that day. I witnessed my child have a vision for something, stick to a plan, and smash her goal with her own effort. It was truly inspirational. After the race, I asked her how was she able to find the gusto to finish so strong? She told me "Dad, I just kept telling myself – PERSEVERE, PERSEVERE, PERSEVERE!". I felt accomplished as a father to have elevated my child to something beyond what she thought she could become. Maybe it was just a 5k to you, but to me it was the very moment I realized how important it is to elevate your child into something greater than yourself.

Chapter 7 | Correction

There is a sense of honor among some men that does not properly convey truth in regard to what disciplinary correction is. It is a very confused perspective that falsely glorifies physical abuse. Men can refer to the way in which they were disciplined when they were as a child as a deserving rite of passage. Tales of being whipped or beaten by extension cords, metal rods, belts, or even pieces of wood have given some young men a false sense of valor or pride. I have witnessed these conversations firsthand that contain this perverted sense of discipline or punishment. "The things my father beat me with" conversations run in the same vein as when youth on a playground debate "whose father could beat whose father in a fist fight". And, those morph with that same fuel to push young men into participating in hazing rituals, whether it be in college or in the military that have even led to inexcusable deaths. There is no honor or valor in physically harming your children. You can make a thousand excuses on why you think it is acceptable, but I can assure you it is not creating the type of growth and connection you need for a strong future relationship. It creates a short-lived false sense of respect, if anything at all.

Patience is the hardest characteristic to develop for a mind that is bent against understanding. If you don't see value in what you seek to improve than the patience to dedicate the time, energy, and effort will not be there. If you are the person who says "nobody tells me how to discipline my kids", I ask you to take a step back, give me a little patience, and allow me to present a different insight to why it is better to offer long-lasting correction rather than short term acts of anger, hostility or whatever you want to call it to your children. I'm not trying to talk you out of spanking your children, I am just informing you that it will not work long term. Because you should never seek to physically harm your children. The fine line is in this question – "where is the blur between punishment, discipline, and correction?" In my opinion, as a parent you can use all three as tactics to promote a positive moral and ethical education. Because, even adults experience all three, just hopefully no longer at the hands of their parents. Years ago, I had a belief that if a bully was punched in the nose it would change his behavior. But since then, I have punched bullies in the nose and learned it did not change their behavior, at least not long term. Under that social/scientific experiment, my hypothesis was proven wrong. But where I have found the most opportunity for change or correction was in demonstrating true conviction and a backbone to face issues head on. Of course, you cannot reason with everyone as some people have ulterior motives and hidden agendas, but you should do your best. It may not correct every situation, but the result is always better than physical violence.

I realize as an adult, I have a responsibility to help my children find different ways of dealing with difficult situations and sometimes it involves our own self-correction. Maybe our own behaviors created a situation that could have been avoided and the outcome was not favorable for anyone. Maybe we couldn't find truth, or distinguish right from wrong, or just couldn't listen. All of which can hopefully be resolved and corrected with time and effort. Try not to be the dad that has to be corrected by his children. It robs them of their innocence.

Truth

From the title of an old 1970 Johnny Cash song, I ask you the question, "What is Truth?" One obvious way you can attempt to explain truth is that it isn't a lie. But really, what is it? I have always told my children that the truth is not always a cute cuddly kitten, it is also a lion that can and will eat you if necessary. It is ferocious and powerful. It is not to be taken for granted. I have worked in sales for several years of my career and I can always remember my dad telling me as a child one day I would be in sales. He was a bit of a prophet in that regard. But I also remember him telling me very early in my life that when I was in that position, I would always be faced with two options, tell the truth or tell a lie. He told me you can't successfully manage both. Incredible wisdom that rings in my ears still today. He helped me to see the value in telling the truth not just now, but later in life. It gave me vision. In your career, you can be presented with opportunities to tell lies to your customers, colleagues or management team anytime you want. Work hard to not do that. When you lie, it enters you into a slippery slope. Lies must maintain lies, slowly building upon a potentially catastrophic house of cards. Integrity isn't cheap and it requires you to face the music. Accountability falters under the weight of lies. Truth starts in you and the value it provides is undeniable.

However, deception is also real. I have observed in my lifetime that those people who constantly harp on specific things in their lives are just revealing their own struggles. I have seen givers steal, marriage counselors found unfaithful, benevolent pastors preach greed, and many free birds caged. Lying to yourself is one thing, but if your actions cause damage to further worsen the lives of others, you must reconsider your behavior and seek to change it. In your job, being labeled as a liar or someone who can't keep their word is quite disruptive and destructive to any team. Even more so if people are depending on you. And if you are a father reading this book, I can assure you people are depending on you. Your actions set the tone for what truth is in the lives of your children. Truth can be defined as operating within the proven or shown facts of any matter. Outside of those bounds lie deception and delusion. And if you're not careful, your behavior will ultimately destroy your valued relationships.

I recently watched a documentary and in it one culture took into consideration of America the belief that we overencourage our children to the point of their own future demise. It was meant in a way that we were not truthful with our children and we often would allow them to believe they are above normal duties or standard expectations for life. The example used was that the American workforce did not perform their work duties as efficiently as the foreign workforce because they viewed this work with less motivation because of their core belief regarding work. Obviously, we do have major cultural differences in our world; right, wrong, or indifferent. The culture who was critical of the American workforce had earlier stated that the only reason we are alive is to work. In my opinion, this too is a form of extremism and lacks proper balance. So, where is the balance in the opposing views? Are we here to teach our children to only have fun or should we have them believe hard work is above them or do we drive them into the ground only believing they are here on earth to work? No, I believe we must seek complete balance. It is about finding a proper life/work balance, not a work/life balance, based on your priorities.

How do you apply balance to anything? You must first observe and then compare against what you already know. If you put others ahead of yourself, especially your children, it becomes easier to find clarity and not see them as a hindrance to your life or goals. They actually begin to become integrated more thoroughly to the way you naturally think. We must be careful to not draw conclusions against our children or think automatically that they make moves with bad intentions in mind. It seems that we often villainize our children because maybe we don't understand them or don't care to. When a father aims to teach his children anything, he must keep in mind that the objective is to correct and help his child to improve his or her future decisions and outcomes. It is not to whack them with something when they make a mistake. Because chances are, they will make more mistakes. A good father always leads with kind and understanding consideration in every situation. Not making excuses for poor choices or behaviors but keeping in mind that you are operating in truth.

Decision-making is part of truth as well. It is one of the most important skills you can teach your children at a very early age. It is how we learn to understand the outcomes of truth. Consequences versus rewards. Consequences can provide painful experiences, but rewards can be quite pleasurable and gratifying. When you are raising children, it is necessary to create opportunities to encourage good decision-making skills. Although as a father there will naturally be plenty to go around, you also want to use your brain and get creative. I am always driven by sharing real world examples that can be impactful for teaching my children. I think our senses serve a greater purpose for learning than what we understand at times. All of your senses can be used to learn and influence your decision making abilities. When you smell a rotten egg, it is quite hard to forget the horrible stench and you probably won't eat it. When you get soap in your eyes, you learn it can burn your eyes and blur your vision and you will probably be more careful next time. When you touch the hot stove, you will burn your hand and you probably won't do that again. When you put a bar of soap in your mouth, you probably won't use bad language. Real world situations, real world decisions.

My wife and I are still in the process of raising children and we believe you must be extremely creative to win in parenting. We have had our fair share of battles with our children. And yes, I said battles, we are in this together, us vs. them, a united front. Battles to have them keep their rooms clean, do their chores, and perform basic hygienic responsibilities. If you have been here, you know how frustrating it can be. We realized very quickly that asking nicely didn't work, yelling didn't work, spanking didn't work, and blaming each other didn't work. (Make sure you listen to that last bit of advice.) We were frustrated and mentally exhausted with the constant day and night asking of our children to complete their required tasks. We were desperate to find a way for them to take ownership of their responsibilities. So, we put our minds together and came up with a plan. We identified the most important item in their individual lives; whether it be a cell phone, bedtime, or story time and decided that these items would be taken away systematically; if necessary. We created a duties chart that displayed a list of their responsibilities and hung it on their bedroom doors. The chart had the days of the week, morning and nightly duties, corresponding duty emojis, and boxes to initial. If the boxes weren't initialed by the end of the day, we wouldn't say a word. Because that was also the other rule; there would no longer be any verbal reminders to do what you were supposed to do. We started this with a family meeting at the dinner table and clearly stated our intentions and that the outcome depended on their own decision-making abilities. They were informed that failure to complete even one of the tasks over the next one-week timeframe would result in a direct consequence on their possessions or lifestyle. For example, if the chart was missing a signature by the "brush your teeth" emoji for the completed week, bedtime moved up 30 minutes. We would begin the next week at the decreased state and if all signatures were in place by the end of the week, the 30 minutes would be restored. If there were three consecutive weeks with all signatures, we would dismiss the chart. But, if responsibilities fell by the wayside again, the chart would appear on the door again. It may seem simple to you, or you may not see yourself doing something like this, and that is fine with me. Just know this. When we implemented this, it changed the way we thought about correcting behaviors in our children. We experienced a difference. We were clear and concise about our expectations and communicated that there would be consequences for failure to do what was required. This gave them the power to understand truth by the simple action of decision making. Observing and acting on the truth does not always produce a physical reward, but it can create an understanding and experience that can help you to avoid the consequences of not doing it. When you are facing a challenging situation with your children, it is important to always follow through with what you say and most importantly, use your noggin.

Balance

Balance is as essential as truth in the life of your children. If you can't receive what they give you, the relationship will not flourish. When you are in the position to teach your children, the consideration and openness you display to them can define your limitations of acceptance for them. They can identify your boundaries to learn as well. Balance is important because they will remember this when it is time to talk about personal aspects in their life. If you knew a simple conversation could have changed a negative outcome in the life of your child, would you have changed your willingness to be more open? I think so. Please consider, because otherwise you'll miss opportunities to be there for them when it counts. I'm not saying just agree with them in everything. No, by all means, feel free to challenge your children. That is what good fathers do. But, never keep the door closed on any discussion in their lives. Life is too short to be unavailable to your children. They deserve nothing but the best from you. When you shut down communication with your children, you risk losing that relationship.

Also important is not dominating them to the point that they can't speak. You are not their drill instructor in the Marines. Meeting them halfway in the relationship is the real balance necessary to allow correction in any situation. The relationship should involve healthy regard for what they have to say also. Your children know when what they say is being authentically contemplated. They know when you are carefully considering what they are experiencing. Sometimes, you should step out of your day to day and remember what it was like to be in their situation. Against better judgment, make yourself vulnerable to feel the pain or heartbreak they say and feel. Find ways to connect with them so that they do not feel alone. Put the relationship into perspective and consider that you only get so many opportunities to do the right thing. And as in much as you would like to think one comment or one talk can fix a situation, think again. It doesn't work that way.

Often, I have found that it is important to meet the energy of their experiences with the same energy. They cannot come to you and say "Dad, my boyfriend just broke up with me." And you just reply with and empty, "well, that's too bad". No, you take the opportunity to show her his loss, not hers. You must find a way to be there for her and help her with your best effort. Too many times fathers may try to avoid these situations, but I think that is a grave mistake. Man up. Father up. Demonstrate to her what love looks like. Help her to find balance in pain. Help her to consider a different perspective in the most loving way you can. The most important tool in a father's wheelhouse is to listen. If you don't have anything insightful to say or even if it isn't necessary, take her out with you somewhere for time alone and just listen. Make time for her. Put things back in balance. Help her to see the light at the end of the tunnel. Be the light in the dark for her. Success in any relationship is the willingness shown to participate in ways that are mutually beneficial to both parties, in both good times and bad.

Sometimes, you may sense a lack of interest from your children, this does not mean it is over. Take time and consider what may be required and don't give up. Many years ago, I coached my oldest daughter in softball. We went through a turbulent time in our relationship, which I know some divorced fathers can easily understand. Coaching her was something I absolutely loved to do. And I could tell it was something she loved as well. We were close during this time, however a rare off-field argument with her mom a day before a very important game made her reconsider our relationship. She arrived at the game and when I tried to greet her, she avoided me. I had never experienced this as a father. She would not even look at me when I spoke to her. I was now considering whether I should just leave the game because of the pure rejection I was feeling. I knew it wasn't the time or place to discuss how she was feeling, so it had to be shelfed and we proceeded to play the game. As this was coach pitch, she requested my assistant coach to pitch to her. This was a move that doubled down on the pain because I was the only person to have ever pitched to her. She was one of our best hitters and I knew exactly where her sweet spot was. A little up and a little inside. She had a habit of turning out and it helped her to make good contact with the ball. But now, I was in an unusual position. I had never watched from the dugout as the kids batted. But there I was. A few innings went on and we were down a few runs. Then one of her teammates told me that my daughter wanted me to pitch to her, because she had already struck out twice. Right before that conversation, I just finished a short prayer. I said, "God I am about to leave this ballpark, unless you please do something now." And I believe with all my heart He did. No one has heard that part of the story. But I feel it's important to note because sometimes you just need a miracle in the mix. I responded to her teammate, "if she wants me to pitch, she is going to have to ask me herself." Another inning went on, we were still down, and she still hadn't asked. Finally, at the beginning of the last inning she stood in front of me and said "Daddy, can you pitch to me?" I humbly nodded "yes". I then hit that field with the enthusiasm and demeanor of an MLB closer. We were down by two runs in the bottom of the 6th inning at the start. She was fourth to bat and I wasn't guaranteed to pitch to her. However, my first two batters got on base with base hits, then my third batter who was quite a speedster hit a double and pushed one run in. Now we were down one run and had runners on second and third. My daughter was now stepping into the batter's box as I fought back tears and realized not only does the team have a chance for winning, but we do too. I stepped on the mound and began to pitch to her. I was quite nervous and threw two bad pitches to start, so 2-0 in the count. I then threw two strikes she didn't hit, so 2-2. The next one was an outside ball, only because she was always picky like me. The legendary full count situation had shown up when everything was on the line. Before my last pitch, I walked halfway to the plate and stuck the ball out towards her and told her "Just like we're in the backyard baby, you got this." I took a deep breath as she stepped in the box. I released the greatest pitch of my life and watched her as she swung and hit it over third base to left field. I turned back to watch her as she rounded first and zoomed on to second base and arrived still standing. With her hit, we won the game as both runners scored. The field cleared and our fans roared, leaving no one on the field except she and I, in what felt like complete silence. There she stood, on top of second base, and I on the pitcher's mound. We immediately ran to each other and she jumped in my arms and I spun her around in the air for what seemed like an eternity. Just she and I in complete celebration of a moment that could have never came if I would have left. In my pain, God absolutely answered my prayer and a valuable lesson in never giving up on my children was learned. And the greatest gift was that I knew the preparation for that moment was already in place. As a boy, I simulated that moment a thousand times in my backyard. Always practicing the scenario of - it's the bottom of the ninth, full count, runners on base, and everything on the line. But I never knew the reason for all of that practice would be just for me and her one day.

Right from wrong

How do you begin to teach your children to determine right from wrong? And how do you arrive at a standard? Obviously, this is where the TRFC principles in the beginning of the book come in. They're the moral parameters we use in our daily interactions with all people. Our culture can also define unhealthy moral norms to our children if we aren't careful. There have been powerfully brave people and countries throughout history that have stood in the face of adversity for the right to fight agendas and campaigns that proudly forced incorrect definitions of right and wrong on people. So, we know even on a global scale the impact that can happen around such a basic topic. But, consider your own home. If you scream at your wife or children and ask them to not do it to others; what do you expect to happen? If you teach them to cheat in life or cut corners, why are you surprised when they cheat on tests in the classroom? When your business practices are questionable, do you really think they see honesty? Not a chance. The greatest factor in teaching a child right from wrong is you. The way you speak, your actions, and your promises are all under the microscope in your children's laboratory. It's really no different than your job, especially if you are managing people. If you manage people and hold them to a standard, don't expect them to not perform it the same way if they catch you doing it incorrectly.

There are some company cultures, regarding discipline and development, that can be summarized by the following two statements. "If you mess up, fess up", and "if you mess up, your fired." I have worked for both in my career. The advantage of the first is that you are promoting a healthy work environment that involves proper training and belief in your employees. The employees are investments. If they make a mistake, they will most likely let you know. If a corrective action is designated, it is normally a joint effort of management and the employee to find a solution and implement it. However, in the second culture, management can become quite distant and removed from the employee relationship. The employees are disposable property that should perform at an expected rate and not make mistakes. This is when you will often hear employees say amongst themselves, I am nothing more than a number at the time clock. I have personally witnessed morale go down when this approach is taken. People begin to worry about what will happen if they make a mistake and are more likely to hide it when something does happen. Then employees adapt and find better ways to hide mistakes or potential issues. There are always behaviors that are easy to see with each management style immediately. But if you don't care, you won't notice.

Most of us have already been through how to cover things up with our parents, so we get it. Think back to when you were a child and that F on your report card grew another leg, and you put a towel over the broken fish tank, or when you hid pillows under your covers to sneak out at night with your friends. No, never mind, that was me… But I am sure you can identify. You know, it was after the shiny halo stage... I am reminded of a time I threw a party at my parents' house while they were out of town. I wish I could blame it on a movie I saw, but I don't think I can. They were gone for the weekend to the beach and I decided it was a fantastic idea to invite my friends over and act like a wild heathen with no home training. However, I do not know where the alcohol came from…. And in court, I do have the right to plead the 5th amendment. Keep that in mind. My parents on the other hand, thought it would be a great idea to come home on Saturday, instead of Sunday, because the weather was going to be bad. A cell phone with the weather app would have come in great back then as a side note. I got the call Saturday morning that they would be home in about an hour. I needed a solid three hours to clean up the mess. Somehow, I managed to clean the house in record time and sit on the couch with my halo polished as they walked in the front door. Weren't they proud? Of course. I was the epitome of a good son. However, I did not account for the fact my dad would go directly to the refrigerator upon arrival and I would instantly remember that I forgot to get the booze out. Uh-oh. He opened the door and my heart was nearly beating out of my chest. He closed the door back and walked into the other room. I panicked and thought maybe now is a good time to go to the gym to play ball or go to a friend's house, but I thought I might look guilty of something. I waited. Then my dad came back in the room and sat down. The silence was killing me. He said, "so, what did you do last night?" Almost if he knew something. I told him "oh, just went to bed early." He saw right through me; everybody knows teenagers don't go to bed early. Then he paused and said "so, who bought the booze?" I am planning my funeral at this point in my mind as I expect to die. I told him "I have no idea and I don't even drink, thaaaattt ummm was my friends..." He remained quiet. Like a silent game of chess, I waited for his move. Then he surprised me. He said, "perhaps you need an education in what alcohol can do to your future." And then he said, "Wednesday night, you will be going to your grandfathers AA meetings." I fought the idea internally, but agreed, because I knew deep down this was my fault and I didn't want to dig a deeper hole for myself. So, for the next two months, I went to my grandfathers' group meetings. There I was, a teenager with twenty grown men talking about all the struggles of their lives and how the shame and pain of being addicted to alcohol brought them to ruin. These men and women told stories of losing their families, jobs, and loved ones. It was truly a learning experience. My dad was a pure genius for exposing me to that firsthand. He completely changed my thinking by exposing me to something I would have likely never seen. These people and my grandfather also changed what I believed about alcohol forever. My dad won the chess match, for sure. And that is the way it is when you are trying to teach your children about right and wrong. They don't want just your opinions; they want to truly believe it or experience it firsthand. At that time, I didn't want to do it, but the lesson stuck with me. My dad didn't know how much it impacted me, but I never threw a party at home again when they were gone; if that means anything... Your real involvement is your best form of correction. That example my father set back then is in my mind as I offer correction to my children today.

Self-discipline

To become an expert in any field, the general consensus is that you need at least 10,000 hours of practice and performance. But what does that consist of? Do you continue to practice the bad habits you learn repeatedly? Or do you learn and employ new habits that allow you to refine your craft? In anything whether it be Karate, hockey, fishing, engineering, or parenting, you are constantly trying to become the best. I had to throw the last one in for this book and for you to see the importance. But, in all of our pursuits of the things we love, we are constantly reading, learning, being instructed to try new things and consider correct ways of doing the things we enjoy. It is in our very nature to improve. I have worked with real experts in various technical fields and what I have found is that they are typically very open to learning. However, if I encounter someone who leads with "trust me, I am an expert," I generally use more caution proceeding. Real experts don't have to advertise they are an expert. I have worked with many PhD's and I always respect that many of them don't disclose that they are highly educated until you realize this person is very knowledgeable in their field.

I don't think we realize the power we give our children to be successful if we can just help them develop self-discipline. From birth we can help them develop proper judgment, situational awareness, and personal growth that can stand alone as they age. After all, they too will most likely become parents one day, just like you. The end game for a father is to teach his children how to eventually self-govern their own personal convictions and understand how the decisions they make daily dictate and influence the paths they choose in life.

One of my most favorite people to have ever lived was George Washington Carver. To preface, he was a scientist, inventor, and incredible human being. He invented over 100 items just from the study and application of what he learned from the peanut. Many of which provide us with items that are common household items that contain plastics, cosmetics, etc. He was a very wise person and worth your time if you get a chance to investigate his life. He is most commonly confused for being the inventor of peanut butter, which is not true, but he did have a real passion to understand it completely. And there is an old quote from GWC worth referencing just on that topic.

"When I was young, I said to God, god, tell me the mystery of the universe. But God answered that knowledge is for me alone. So, I said, god, tell me the mystery of the peanut. Then God said, well, George, that's more nearly your size." GW Carver.

As a young boy, he loved to draw. As slaves, his family was too poor to afford drawing materials for art. So, he made his own. He mixed berries, moss, and bark to formulate paints. He practiced his art by sketching plant foliage and scenes from nature. He would even use his materials from the plants to draw the same plants. That idea is quite beautiful and from the heart of a true conservationist for sure. He studied botany first and learned agriculture next. He became an expert in both fields. Later he went on to study chemistry and become a professor at Tuskegee University. He was behind the idea and implementation of crop rotation, which helped the soils in the south to recover nutrients from season to season and avoid the destruction of the infamous boll weevil. Carver went on to be an advisor to President Theodore Roosevelt and even Gandhi regarding agriculture, nutrition, and other topics. Being one of the most highly respected scientists and African Americans in the country, he was highly sought after and constantly working to improve upon the developments he had discovered. So, accomplishment after accomplishment, he always stayed true to his work. The real heart of George Washington Carver was exposed to me by the statement he made regarding why he never married. He said, "no woman could ever be happy with a man that had to get up every morning to speak to the plants for two hours to start the day." A beautiful picture of unwavering self-discipline that very few of us have.

If by chance our interactions, small daily corrections, and examples can influence our children in a positive meaningful way, we can unashamedly say we have done our best to leave the world better than we found it. It is your service to your children to teach them to think, discover, and lead the life they will be proud of. And in that, I leave you with one more quote from GWC that I believe is quite fitting in context of this book.

"It is not the style of clothes one wears, neither the type of automobile one drives, nor the amount of money one has in the bank, that counts. These mean nothing. It is simply service that measures success."

Chapter 8 | Teach

To uncover the deeper value and meaning for this chapter, we need to start by looking at our history as a nation. Do you realize that we are only around 80 years out from the FSLA child labor laws enacted by President Roosevelt that really changed us as a nation? For everyone reading this book, it is extremely likely that your grandparents or great grandparents experienced this transition firsthand. We have had US Presidents Hamilton and Jefferson believed in the value and importance of child labor. And it is not the type of labor you are thinking of. Maybe at first you are thinking of a kid in a drive thru window taking your fast food order. No, not that kind. The children I'm referring to here were as young as four and worked hard labor and long hours in mills, mines, and factories across the country. If you want a good read, spend some time on the US Bureau of Labor Statistics. The stories are quite egregious and tell the true story of the millions of children who helped build the United States during the industrial revolution. I have read different estimations that children across the country under the age of twelve would have easily accounted for 30-40% of the income generated for a household. Even today, it is predicted that over 150,000 young children are still forced into child labor here in the States. And yet, t is not uncommon for us as a nation to look down our nose at foreign countries who practice child labor abuse. But even more reason why we need to do our research. Why would prior US Presidents or anyone support the idea that children should be forced into the industrial workforce and expect them to contribute as adults? One would assume it was just because times were hard, and it was "necessary". But there was also an overwhelming idea at the time that if children were left with idle time, they would most likely become a vagabond or criminal, in other words. And hard labor was viewed as a minor transition for most children because many of them had been so accustomed to life on the farm and the chores that were required there. It is important to keep this in perspective as we get to the second part of the intro for this chapter.

During this time, there were also many people pushing to offer education for children as well. And of course, as you can imagine, they had vested interests in what the curriculums were and the amount of time the children could spend in class. Public education has been around in the US for much longer than the 19th century. The very first classrooms can be traced back to the Puritans of the original thirteen colonies. The Puritans had objectives to teach the Bible personally, because they were Protestants and believed it was important to be able to read and understand the Bible for matters of faith. The workforce at the turn of the 20th century was growing and the push for tailor made education was intensifying. The industry was demanding curriculums that provided children with necessary trade skills to perform well at their jobs. So, in many cases, children were going to school and had to work all day. I don't believe most Americans are truly aware of how recent and how bad these situations were for children. And then on top of that influence you had a real fight amongst educators about how to teach them. Should the children be taught to memorize information to later regurgitate in the form of a test or should they be taught from a "hands on, pragmatic approach?" I appreciate the diplomatic insights of the late Professor John Dewey who stated *"The business of the teacher is to produce a higher standard of intelligence in the community, and the object of the public school system is to make as large as possible the number of those who possess the intelligence. Skill and ability to act wisely and effectively in a great variety of occupations and situations is a sign and a criterion of the degree of civilization that a society has reached. It is the business of the teacher to help in producing many kinds of skills needed in modern life. If teachers are up to their work, they also aid in the productions of character. (Dewey, TAP, pp. 241-242)* At the time, these were incredible insights to what the greater purpose was, whether he knew it or not, because for the first time the actual child was considered an individual.

An education can free you and give you opportunities not previously possible. In our modern life, we have many more options for fields of study that our children can now pursue. Our children's opportunities are most likely the greatest they have ever been in the history of our country. The message of this chapter is to make sure you don't take that for granted. It is our responsibility to help our children achieve the best education possible. That doesn't mean we just pay for a fancy private school, take our hands off the wheel and hope for the best. No, in fact it is completely opposite. It means you take the responsibility for the education they receive, and you do everything you can to help them develop into what they were born to be.

Get involved

Have you ever changed a flat tire? Did you get your hands dirty? Of course, you did. That is a chore that is almost impossible to do without getting dirty. Changing a tire is easy work if you have the right tools. It is an essential 101 course lesson that every father must teach his children. It is even better if you can ask them what to do in case things don't go as planned. Imagine your child just called you with a flat tire and they are stuck on the side of a busy highway and borderline panicking. The bad news is that you didn't teach them how to change a flat. What would you do? Maybe just email them an instructional video? Heck no. You get in the car and drive there as fast as you can to make sure they are safe, and you get the tire changed. I know some of you are thinking I would just call the insurance company to go out and fix it, but I would hope you wouldn't do that to your kid in their time of need. You don't get many opportunities to come to the rescue, don't miss out on those. So, when you pull up, you may not have time to teach them what must be done, so you just get the job done. It is what you do as a dad. Once the job is completed and everyone is safe and accounted for, you go back to work or home and your child goes on their way. But now, you need to think about how I can make this situation better next time. What can I do to help them not panic? One of the greatest things you can do is empower them by giving them the knowledge and ability to do something they didn't know how to do before. And keep in mind that practice makes perfect. I know as a seasoned dad or coach you also have said that at least a thousand times. You now take them to a safe spot you can work on changing a tire and you make learning this lesson a priority. Changing a tire is one of those things that is almost impossible to teach without getting involved. I have taught two of my five children how to change a tire by now. It took time and patience on my side. For them it took attention and action. Handling a tire is quite a dubious task, because it is big and somewhat of an awkward shape. But again, having the proper tools can equip you to get things done very proficiently. Learning how to pick a tire up and line it up with very little effort eliminates half the struggle of changing it. This is where we learn the value of using a tool that can become a lever. These are the types of things dads are made of. I love to see the light go off in my children's eyes when they discover something new to them and they understand. It is the famous aha moment.

Parenting is not a spectator sport. It involves creativity and ambition if you plan to do it well. The pragmatic approach to parenting is my favorite method. When you get to participate in something together that challenges you both, you are most likely to bond on a greater level than if you just barked out orders to do something. And that doesn't include just the things that are exciting either. It means in the very mundane as well. I know you may have limits on the topics you feel capable to handle, but that is part of the satisfaction that is provided when you do something together. Trust me, it will never be done in vain. You will not lay down on your death bed one day and say, "I really wish I hadn't got involved with you on that Spanish test when you were studying in 9th grade." If anything, that will be a memory that lives on in the mind of your child that you went above and beyond the call of duty for.

Currently two of my children are in the middle school band and this is completely foreign territory for me. I am hearing new words like "woodwinds, crescendos, staccatos, and bugattos", on the regular. Not sure the last one is a real word. But for me to be involved in the conversation, I am now required to do a little bit of studying. When I take the time to understand this new lingo, I find that they really have some interesting perspective on what they hear when I am just hearing something that sounds like organized noise. Both the music and what they are saying begins to make sense. I am not crowding them out, but I am showing them I care about the things they are learning, and I want them to excel, so I am at the ready to step up and help anytime I can. I want to get my hands dirty when possible, but I know I lack in the musical rhythm necessary, so playing an instrument is out of the question. I know my limitations, but I will make up for it in other more creative ways. Because I love them and want them to know I care about them and the things they are interested in. You may not like volleyball, science, or homework, but it is highly worth it to pick up a brand new interest.

Self-discovery

It took Thomas Edison over a thousand times to fail before finally finding success with the invention of the light bulb. Imagine if he would have given up for good. We would be using candles today. And that is the heart of self-discovery; not giving up. At times we feel that we should just quit and lay down. But we get back up again. When you are teaching your children about life, it is important to always begin anything you do with the mindset that we may fail, but we will not give up. I have always told my children that if you begin something or commit to it, you will see it through. If that means it is a season of a sport or a four-week class, we will see it through. The strength of the human soul is in our ability to not give up. When your child is hungry to explore new avenues of learning or to find out if they just like something, it cannot be reiterated enough to push them to do their best and never give up. I can assure you with all the options children have today, you can easily help them find what they love.

But, why is it that we give up? Is it from a lack of encouragement or is it just because something is just deemed too hard to complete? Maybe we underestimated the cost and commitment? Maybe we feel as though we can't do it? Many questions cloud my mind in why we give up and walk away from the things we may consider enjoyable. Careful consideration for your children will help you to identify why they want to give up on new explorations. Sometimes, it can be influence from friends or others. It is important to offer help to them when you see them attempting to quit something. Probably more important than when you encourage them to try something new. Starting something new is easy, quitting on the second day is even easier according to author Jon Acuff, writer of the book "Finish". He recently stated on social media that more people give up on his 30-day challenge on the second day by a much higher percentage than any other. That is quite interesting. You would think they would at least give more effort; maybe like day fifteen or later. And these are adults, who always finish what they start.... How much more should we encourage our children to finish what they start. This conversation starts in the home and it is a trait that can be developed. I could pour out hundreds of stories of what it means to not give up and give countless examples of people who sacrificed or gave everything to attain something for themselves or the ones they loved, but I won't. You, like all of them have the chance to help your children not only explore what they like or love, but also learn lessons about themselves and define their own interests, in spite of wanting to give up.

Self-discovery is also a valuable aspect of personal exploration. Your child may find themselves participating in sports, clubs, or events that they really may not be interested in at all. Help them to find the truth in that if you perceive it. It could save their life later. Following the crowd without someone to help you can sometimes cause you to lose your direction and identity. Safeguard the exploration of your children's life. Not that they live in a bubble, but make sure their decisions are their own, and that they demonstrate personal conviction when looking to change any situation. I believe when that behavior is left unchecked it can grow into bad behavior that causes them to not be able to find a firm footing on life. Partaking in drugs and alcohol are always done in this mode of exploration. If you have high schoolers, don't be naïve to the daily interactions they are confronted with. It is not uncommon that drugs and alcohol use even starts in middle schools. As you also know, we are in an opioid epidemic in this country. Pills are unassuming and may land in the hands of your children as simple as they land in your medicine cabinet in your home. In the name of self-discovery or exploration, kids can partake in very deadly behaviors. We have heard the stories of children strangling themselves because they decided to play games they heard about at school. They need you to be there and having the necessary conversations to ask the pertinent questions about their lives. You are not a mind reader, but you must stay current with what could or could not be going on with them.

Adventure

Beauty is in the eye of the beholder, so they say. It is all truly about perspective. One of my favorite Will Smith movies is

"The Pursuit of Happyness." And yes, that is the correct spelling of the movie title. Also noted is the fact that it was based on a true story about the life of Chris Gardner. In one scene from the movie, the main character is homeless with his son and they lived in Downtown San Francisco. One night when they were not able to sleep at the shelter, they found themselves on a bench in the subway. The father, with nowhere else to go, decided to begin acting like he heard dinosaurs and convinced his son that they must find a cave. The cave was the unoccupied public restroom. His young son never knew any different and they stayed the night in the floor near the door inside the restroom. They were both obviously in a very tough situation, but his dad, in his pursuit of happiness, did whatever it took to make this a fun adventure for his son. He helped to form an experience and memory in the mind of his young son that helped even him escape the reality of the situation they were in. He changed his perspective. And really isn't that what adventure does. When you go on vacation to distant places, you own that beach for the weekend, you own that lake, and you own that condo. Or at least that is the way you feel. After the week or weekend has worn off, your money is gone and the reality sets in that you didn't own it after all. However, in the moment you felt removed from the stress you felt at work or just in life in general. And in the end, if you did it right, you were able to enjoy the time and reset your mind to feel refreshed and renewed. Adventure can lead to transformation, if you allow it. New experiences shape who we are becoming. We learn what we like and dislike. Your children have a hunger for adventure. Whether it is going out to climb a tree in the backyard or a camping trip, they are excited by the opportunities to be inquisitive and discover. It is important to remember that we are helping them to find things they enjoy, and adventure is a very useful tool in that toolbox.

As a young man I worked on developing a specialized skill set for about ten years. I thought this trade would be what I wanted to do for many years to come. I succumbed to being dissatisfied with the company culture and role I was involved with. I decided it was time to leave and start a new career. I was young and green in my decision making, but I had passion and vision. In my heart I knew I could find something else that would make me happy again. I had the full support from my wife to leave and find something else. It took a little time, but I found a new job to begin my career. It was completely different than my previous responsibilities. I found myself starting again from the bottom, but I took the challenge head on. It is very important to preemptively note that during my job interview with this new company I did not mention my previous working experience in detail, because I didn't see it as valuable as I was taking a position as a general laborer. I went from an office job to a role now that included very physical labor. I tried hard to prove myself and do the best job I could. In six months, I was promoted to a supervisor role. Fast forward a year, and I am sitting in my office contemplating my position of supervisor. I enjoy it and I find it very rewarding as I am meeting my goals and helping my guys to meet theirs as well. But I had a moment. A moment I will never forget. I sat there in a quiet office and just briefly considered all the history and experience I had with my previous skill set, that I did miss at times, and asked God one simple question – "Was all of that experience in vain?" Then in that fleeting moment, someone walked in and I snapped back into work mode. Two weeks later I came in to punch the clock and saw a job posting on the board for a specialist in a certain field that was seven hundred and fifty miles away from where we lived. The company would post job openings at other plants and always try to promote from within. It was one of their founding principles. That certain field of expertise just so happened to be my field of expertise and was a completely new direction for this company. They had no one across the entire group of the company who knew anything about this field. But me. I had chills the day I read that job posting. You could have printed my resume and laid it side by side against the job posting and it was almost identical to what they wanted. I immediately called my wife and asked her what she thought about moving across the country. She answered with "let's go!" Because she is awesome. I had begun speaking about the job as if it was automatically mine. The next thing I did was find articles I had written for magazines and whitepapers I did for other companies to use pertaining to this field. I sent them to the job poster and the Director of Engineering. I may have even sent them to the VP of the company as well. I was a little excited to say the least. Our passions rise to the top without asking them to. No one I worked with had a clue about my past job experience or any of the things I had knowledge of because it did not matter in the line of work I was now part of. The next week I received a phone call and it was the Engineering Director letting me know that he wanted to review my resume'. He flew down two weeks later for a follow up interview and to discuss the position. Two more weeks went by and the VP flew down to meet me and told me that the job was mine, and that HR would arrange the move and make it seamless. But only under one condition, he told me I could not answer his offer until the end of the week. He wanted me to make sure my wife and family agreed before committing. So, I went home, and we had a family meeting to discuss this new adventure we were now faced with. At the time, my wife and I had three children. One of those three was my oldest daughter from a previous marriage. She did not live with us at the time. My two youngest at the time have the same spirit of adventure like my wife and were two very fast "yes's". And with all the truth in my heart, I can honestly tell you that it all rode now on the response of one person, our oldest daughter. She and I both knew that if I took this job, we couldn't see each other the way we always had. I felt overwhelmed at the thought of telling her that if she wanted me to stay, I would. I was fully prepared to do so. That is what dad's do. So, there I sat, waiting for her reply. She looked at me and said something no one else could. She said "Dad, this is a once in a lifetime opportunity, you have to take it." I admired her maturity, wisdom, and acceptance. I promised her that I would do everything in my power to keep and maintain our close connection. And I did. I drove or flew seven hundred and fifty miles one way for the next five years, every month, to make sure she knew I would never abandon her. It wasn't easy, but it was worth it. Her unwavering acceptance and approval pushed us to step out in faith. I had the entire family on board as a complete decision. We make our decisions as a family. To finish the story, I let the VP know that Friday and we began the process immediately.

As we were packing, I felt reminded of the question I asked God and I realized the things that happened in my life were not in vain, not even my mistakes. It felt like the adventure was just beginning and I was so happy to have my family to share it with. When my youngest two started their new school, I reminded them that they were brilliant at making friends and that is exactly what they did. They made a ton of friends and had all kinds of new experiences. They missed home at times, just like I did, but we worked it out together, because that is what families do. In the beginning, we had some family and friends that weren't excited about us leaving our hometown and I understand. But through the eyes of adventure, it taught me valuable insight. Not everyone will be pleased or understand the road you must take to be true to yourself but only you can help your children understand.

I always instruct them to not be judgmental of people who don't have the same sense of adventure, but always consider that everyone is on a different journey and that adventure can be defined in many ways. And one of the biggest things they remind me of often is that by moving they made more friends and connections and it has enriched the experience. Especially because they never really lost the friends they had, they just added more. It really helped them to not be afraid of change as well. And for some people, change can be the most frightful thing in a situation, whether they can admit it or not. I want to raise my children to not be afraid of taking risks and if one day they live across the world when they grow up, so be it. I will know that I have given them plenty of preparation, power, and mindset to do whatever they want to do. And with that, I want you to realize that adventure is freedom.

Chapter 9 | Inspire

Last year over the summer I found myself emerged in business travel and it brought me near some unbelievable destinations. I have a personal rule to not just stay in the room on travel, but I believe you should always go explore if you have the time. So, over that spectacular month I experienced the sunrise over the prolific mountain range of the Swiss Alps while I was cruising on the Autobahn, the sun setting in the living panoramic painting of the Yosemite Valley, looked up from underneath the Giant Sequoias in the Valley of the Giants, I walked the streets of Strasbourg in all of its full spring beauty and vibrant colors, and felt the mist and power from the millions of gallons of water churning over the edge of Niagara Falls. While taking in all these marvelous sights and experiences, I thought to myself these must be moments of sheer inspiration. But were they? I left in complete awe and felt something I couldn't quite put in the adequacy of words. But I didn't invent anything that impacts the experience of humanity or discover any new cures for detrimental health conditions common to humanity upon my return. Maybe that really happens or maybe that only happens in movies, the jury is out.

Finding the true definition amongst scholars and psychologists of inspiration is a little more complicated than it first appears on the surface. There are many good studies done on the topic, but it seems safe to say inspiration comes from a unique personal impact created by an experience, a physical object, or an individual. Inspiration undeniably stirs our soul and compels us to change or improve our lives or those around us. And fundamentally in reference to move us to what we consider a marginally better state of being. It is not hard to find in most organizations today, people teaching about leadership and trying to call out the "greatness" in their employees, students, or clergy. With the intrinsic questions revolving around better performance, labeled as, "greatness". The way I am defining greatness is to bring out the best in an individual for the greater cause of the group or organization. Solidarity and understanding of greatness are defined by the individual and only sought once there has been a realization of value and gain that comes from the attainment of such. And that is the basic mechanics of inspiration.

But for now, let's look at how many of these classes or leadership courses go about business. Managing people is quite a difficult task. Why? People have free will, emotions, preexisting relationships, commitments, and a value system that weigh in on all of the decisions that they make. An organization may bring someone in to teach a group of employees "how to be better leaders", but what they are intending to do as their primary function is inspire and equip for better performance. It is at the heart of every class or course that is held with development in mind. And in theory that should work, but if the conviction of the individual is based on jaded personal experience, they will buck most of the "feel good" aspects that are promoted in these sessions. For example, if an employee has had a past experience of someone being hired to take their place and being told to train them, it is going to be quite difficult to teach or inspire this person to become more open with their colleagues; no matter how clever you think you are. Here in the real world, they realize the trainer quickly exits the picture and they are back in the cutthroat world of management/employee relations they have come to know and have complete disdain for. Which leaves them hardly equipped or inspired. I have been through countless trainings and have never seen a time when relationships were discussed or put on the mend. And without strong relationships, it is difficult for a person to even be willing or open to any change.

I think watching children naturally interact and negotiate gives us better insight for how to achieve true inspiration and lessons on life. In your mind, you may think it would be like the "Lord of the Flies", but this couldn't be further from the truth. Most children are compassionate and considerate. I am reminded of times early in my working career when I would carry stress home. At night, I would tuck my daughter in bed, and we would pray together. I would always pray first and then afterwards, she would pray. Considering her prayers, mine were very robotic and didn't really leave much room for hope. She would always start hers out with "Thank you God for this beautiful day." Once inspired with what I heard from her, it compelled me to forever change the way I pray. Even to this day, when I pray, I begin with "Thank you God for this beautiful day." Then I make all my complaints known…. not really.... But you get the point. Life is too short to allow stress to dictate your perception. Kids can help you get it right.

Professionals have a much harder time in trying to convey to us why we should believe or try to reach for something different. Perspective is what really changes when inspiration comes along. I'm not saying leadership courses or classes are not ok. What I am saying is that many times they lack the true authenticity and genuineness humans need to apply healthy changes and to sustain new behaviors. And you as a father have this great opportunity as you interact daily with your children. The way you choose to inspire your children is up to you. But, I would rather you try to help them find new ways and roads to greatness than push them down the stairs like many people in the world are waiting to do in only just a short matter of time. And even if they do get pushed down, be the one to help them up. And most importantly, allow your children room to inspire you. It is perfectly ok with them if you don't know everything. I want to spend this chapter expressing what I think inspiration means in reference to the interactions and relationship you will share throughout your life with your children. I may not cover it all, but I hope something I write will inspire you to think differently and cause you to pursue better.

Example

Your actions are your children's greatest forms of inspiration. The way you treat your spouse, your parents, your job and how well you keep your word directly impact the level of inspiration they can receive from you. But really, it's not only your actions, it is also the insight and clarity you give them on how they view life and those around them. Kids are masters at detecting hypocrisy and calling out those discrepancies in the way they have been informed to behave versus the way they see demonstrated. Your passion, persistence, attitude, and authenticity are constantly under scrutiny. Until, they see something great in you. It may be one act, or it may take fifty years to see it clearly. You may be here, or you may be gone, but if you do the great things, the inspiration will come.

Many great artworks and inventions lack praise until much later into their existence as well. It is easy to lose count of the stories of great artists and inventors who were not received well during their prime. Every day, you can display your commitment and consistency to your children. I am reminded of my 86-year-old grandmother who has provided me with great aspirations and long-lasting inspiration. I am nearing forty years old and cannot remember one year that has gone by that I have not received a birthday card and a ten-dollar bill from my grandmother. And she always takes the time to write a special note too. So, in total, that is almost $400 bucks over my lifetime from her. She has also done this for her four children, their spouses, her grandkids, and her great grandkids as well. Keep in mind that some of the great grand kids are nearly twenty years old and we have a large family. That is a fair sum of money, but it is much more than that. When she turned 75, we all decided that we would give her ten dollars from every family member as a gift. I think we all were proud of that idea and the consideration was paramount to most things we collectively considered doing. However, she wasn't taking this lightly. While she greatly appreciated the gesture and she obviously wasn't in need of the $400 or so, it was her response that taught me something more about what it means to be inspirational. After she opened it, she looked around the room and told everyone thank you. It was quite touching. Shortly after, she told most of us individually the following, "Thank you all again for this gift, and while I appreciate it, I just want you to know that this money will not be spent. It will be sent to you on your birthday within the first year of my passing." I couldn't believe she out-loved us. But then again, it was just like her to teach us about what it means to love. This was a real moment of inspiration. Her full authenticity on display for all of us to see. This is what it means to pass down a legacy. Real inspiration produces a response that propels us into a better future.

Maybe for you it's not about the things I am discussing. Maybe it boils down to just staying clean. Your fight for sobriety will be much more appreciated by your children than just walking away and leaving them with pain or abandonment. In consideration to the safety and wellbeing of your children, I must mention that if you are struggling with an addiction, you must do everything you can to get help and prevent your children from experiencing the pain that comes along with that lifestyle. It is extremely difficult to find inspiration when a child's innocence is being compromised by the actions of his or her parents. Dr. James Dobson holds a special place in my heart as being a man of integrity who has worked very diligently to promote the value of family and the role of both mother and father and the responsibility they both share in protecting the innocence of a child. I find this to be my greatest cause and effort in allotting my children the chance to enjoy the only childhood they will have in this life. It is quite the responsibility when you think about it.

You can try hard today to protect your children but can feel completely helpless and under attack by simple entertainment choices disguised as fun and easy-going. Don't let your guard down as a father. If you have personal convictions as a father, stick to them. I shared an earlier story that my wife and I work hard to not allow certain forms of entertainment in our home. We have that right as parents. We have received criticism in the past for being too strict by others, but we try hard to take even those comments into consideration. We believe in balance first and foremost. Especially in the weighing out of truth. We believe that it is contradictory to teach your children the value of family and loving one another but allow movies and music that are in complete opposition to those values. If I and my wife are to give the example of what a marriage is to look like, how can we allow our children to view or even learn to enjoy things that promote infidelity or physical violence against one another. We do not model a perfect marriage, far from it. We both have our own shortcomings, faults, and disagreements. But we are real, and we are authentic. To say that I will be inspired to change the world by seeing a beautiful sunset is as shallow as saying my children won't be influenced by the superficial realities given out to the masses in America through most of the modern entertainment industry. We refuse to allow our children to be a byproduct of the disarmament of the family unit by modern culture; whether they realize they are doing it or not. Buying into the reality that is sold today teaches children that it is ok to disrespect their parents and see no value in anything other than self. If you don't believe me, spend time and study what is out there in high supply and demand in opposition of the traditional family. I am not saying go hide under a rock and hope everything is better when you come out, but I am pointing out what you are up against when trying to offer your children the best shot at an inspired future.

Hope is the source of all inspiration. I believe that because if you have a thought of inspiration, it is always weighed out against what you see as your current reality versus what you believe is possible; even if you have some doubt. When we learn that our parents are not dependable or even worse, that they can't be trusted, we can be much more likely to stop believing in the hope that things can change. This isn't really about optimism or pessimism either. The glass isn't half full or half empty. I don't want to paint a picture of the intangibles or the unreachable. I want you to consider the honor and privilege you have by affording your children the platform to imagine and create the world in the only way that their own unique beliefs can. Checks and balances are an important part of providing that fruitful platform and not allowing the world to squelch the ideas of inspiration they have. In the measure of a child's inspiration, it is far better to be the person to help them see the reality thought through and without crushing their dreams. When you crush a child's thoughts as a parent in a world that is already so hard to be heard in, you are doing them a great disservice. It is not uncommon to hear children say that when they grow up, they want to be just like their dad. Moms get love too, but just trying to help you understand what's at stake here. If your child is willing to model their life after yours, is there really a greater opportunity for inspiration? If you can realize now that all you do sets forth the example for what type of future is achievable, you will be far better for it in the years to come. To be an example to your children is the greatest privilege a man can possess to ensure they don't miss out on the most important aspects of life.

Connect

Setting the example of being a hard worker is important, but the upgrade is in the ability to open and share what that means. As any good father has done, you have brought your children into countless projects and chores. But do you ever just do something with them to let them see the mechanics of how you work or give them insight into how you view certain topics. For example, your children may know what you do as an occupation, but do they know what you really do. Have you ever taken them to work and explained something? I know it may not be possible to take your kids to work or you may work in such a high-level environment you can't share it. But what is important is that you make time for your kids without the demands of feeling like something must be delivered. You may work on a project together that doesn't really mean much in terms of productivity or even meet building codes and standards. But that is the point. Never consider that to be wasted time. Sometimes as men, we skip over the experience and look for the result. If I have learned anything as a father, this must be one of my greatest lessons. For the first ten years or so as a dad, I felt as if I had to rush through every project and get it done in record time. I no longer see it this way. If I have a project that doesn't involve an emergency, I am very intentional to make sure I find the time to include my children in some aspect. Sometimes individually and sometimes together, it depends on the project. To see their eyes, light up as we complete a task or when they discover a new trick to do something better really brings me joy.

I worked as a design engineer for a few years and my favorite part of designing was to see the final product. One Saturday I asked my boss if I could take my daughter to the office and show her how to use a design software. She was still in high school and I was trying to give her some exposure and connect with her more to help her define her interests. I knew how much I enjoyed the process of designing and thought maybe she would as well. So, it's not that easy to just go in and draw a picture of something and hit print. Especially if it is a version of something in front of you that you can see or hold. There are certain things that you must learn before you can understand what you are doing. I sat down at my desk with her and we took a small metal plate that had a few holes and radiused corners. I told her that this was her project for the day. She would make a 3d model and it would be just like the one in her hand. I taught her what calipers were and how they were necessary for us to determine the measurements of the part and without them, we couldn't recreate the part. Then we took our paper out and made a quick sketch of what the parts outline or shape was. I taught her about dimensioning a part and why it was important to know the location of features on a component. I also showed her why it was important to look at the part from multiple angles and how a part was to be rotated in terms of a blueprint and that there were preexisting standards for how this was to be done. Now we had a general understanding of the how and why for design. She measured the part and wrote her measurements down between the arrows used for dimensioning and then measured the thickness. Then once completed, she turned to the computer and begin to transfer that same sketch onto the screen within the 3d modeling software. I sat behind her as she entered her information on the screen for dimensions. What a perfect seat for a dad. She finished her dimensional sketch and now it was time to give it a material thickness; which design engineers call an extrusion. This is where the magic happened. The moment she extruded the sketch, I instructed her to rotate the part and she turned around with such an amazing look of shock in her eyes as she proclaimed, "I made that?!?" I said, "Yes, you did!" She was so proud that she created something. As a father I had seen firsthand that the simple connection I made by sharing my world with her made her feel completely inspired by something most of us would so easily take for granted. That part on my desk no longer held just a place in this world as a mechanical bracket, it was now something I would never forget. It was where I saw the light of inspiration in the eyes of my child. Take the time to intentionally connect with your children, even if you don't see it as productive. There is much more going on in that moment than you realize.

Future

Long lasting impact and influence is not superficial and it's not cheap. There is a cost with being a good father. Sometimes it can cause you to miss that promotion or that outing. I have seen mindless motivation pumped into employees in terms of shallow incentives. A little piece of cheese or a dangling carrot is all they ever really are. Just enough to get you to the next month and make sure you are meeting the demands of what is expected of you. Man, that statement may not be received well, but, nonetheless. Understand that I am not writing this book for you to become a better employee, but a better father. I want you to see that your short-term actions are projecting you into the future that will determine itself as a result. Work is not your priority. It is merely a means to provide for your family. You are the one who buys into whether you measure success by how your employer or industry feels about you. Your children will never sit down with you at the dinner table and ask you how you impacted the company today. We can be brainwashed into chasing that next title or position to a default. I ask you to check your motivations. When a man can be honest with himself, he can gain his true freedom. I didn't say compare himself. Maybe your motivation for that new position is to be able to afford the car the neighbors just bought across the street. Work hard, enjoy your career, but check your ego and don't let it get in the way of your children. Their future depends on it and so does yours. Your achievements and accolades are fleeting in comparison to what really matters. Take the future into consideration when dealing with your children. Let them know that you plan to be an integral part of it. How can you do that today? Inspire them with the future.

Every year we celebrate New Year's Eve as a family at our dinner table. We drink champagne and the kids have sparkling grape juice served from long stem glasses and make it a bit of a gala affair. We fancy it up a little bit. Over the evening, we enjoy a nice meal, nice music, and casual conversation. After dinner we anticipate the spectacular. For almost ten years, we have sat down to do our "ACE event, (Annual Commemoration of Expectations)". We review our written past expectations experienced and plan our future expectations. But it is so much more than that. The format consists of nine different categories. I have listed them below with a brief description for each one.

ACE 20** - Annual Commemoration of Expectations

1. Impact person of the year – a person who has made us view life in a more positive way or possibly changed the course for the better because of the encounter and influence.

2. Impressive memory of the year – an experience that summarized or shaped the year into what it became, or the reason it was otherwise unforgettable.

3. What we're thankful for – our respect and consideration for the often overlooked things in life

4. Tribute to family lost – a time for us to write a short commentary on a person we lost and to give honor or tribute to their memory to allow us to preserve in our minds who they were

5. Achieved expectations – review of the expectations we set in the prior year and whether we reached them

6. New expectations – new expectations and ideas to implement for the year to come

7. What we learned about ourselves – the reality of the year summarized

8. Past year reflection word – the word that we intend to shape our future, our focus word

9. New year reflection word – our focus word for the future that may be what we want to improve on or build our expectations around

This event for our family yields healthy portions of laughter, tears, joy, and sometimes pain. It is what we truly look forward to at the end of the year. After we have examined the experience of the year, we often spend the rest of the evening reflecting on the years prior. Which only build up what we believe about ourselves and inspire us to reach for more than we think possible. I felt that years ago, new year's resolutions were too empty of a thing to think for a second they contained any life changing power. This has proven to be a much better choice. The depth in which we connect and look forward to one another's own personal story is unmatched. It is the culmination of our family experience. This book is really the only time I have shared this, except it be with a few close friends or family members. My vision for it is that it continues to be passed down as a tradition in our family to my children, my children's children and so on. That is my hope. I know it can't be guaranteed, but I know for now it really matters. And if there be any value for you in this sharing of our ACE event, please by all means, introduce your own version that fits your family and allows your children to aspire to higher expectations and experiences. File these types of experiences in your minds in the "un-regrettable" section.

Chapter 10 | Encourage

Belief in another human being is one of the most life-giving transactions that can be communicated. The countless hours we spend as parents in just building up a belief system for our children can be quite daunting. The lengths we go to help them believe they are capable and worthy of being a part of something bigger than themselves is played on a repeat cycle throughout the entirety of the relationship. I can see children being dropped off for the first day of kindergarten and the first day of college, still in need of that belief from their parents. I can see that little boy playing his first day of youth baseball and his first day of signing with a Major League team, still in need of that belief from his parents. I can see that little girl holding her daddy's hand as he walks her into her first dance and I can see him walking her down the aisle, still in need of that belief from her daddy. Some things never change. Even as life progresses. The assurance and belief you provide as a father is palpable in the life of your children. You may have moments that you think you don't impact their thoughts or decisions, but I can assure you that is not the case. You play one of the most important roles in their lives. And one of the most important responsibilities you have is to help them know someone will never leave them alone. And that message of encouragement is an unwavering, unrelenting, and unchanging effort to always be there, no matter the cost. As I have said before, you don't get to opt out. There is no bankruptcy, no divorce, and no default.

I am not a big fan of pep talks when it comes to shallowness or superficiality. I have seen unbelievable efforts put into trying to convince people to completely over commit themselves to things that will not matter for long. Sales goals that drive men to become things they didn't believe possible in the name of growth, workers risking their lives in the name of deadlines and manpower, and managers willing to sacrifice their families in the name of success. That is the opposite of encouragement, it is discouragement. And that is what your children feel every time they feel like they were put on the backburner. I really don't want to come across as I am against labor or working, but I feel we are in dire need to understand what's at stake here. We meet far too many people that can't see it.

The questions have been asked time and time again. What profits a man to gain the world and lose his soul? Do you realize what your soul is? It is not just you. It is everything about you. Your family is the larger portion in that equation. Sometimes to reach the heart of encouragement, you must break down the walls that are holding back the message. We block out what we truly want to just keep the convenience. Change is admittedly the hardest part. Several years ago, I was involved with a project that required me to work over 3400 - 3600 hours a year in consecutive years. Keep in mind, the average hours worked per year in the US, according to a recent Forbes article, is around 1600 – 1800, depending on the industry. I was willing to double that consistently in the name of project success. I had a real belief that this is what was required to be successful. Not just my success, but for the success of the company. It had grown outside of my own mind to something I could not reign in or put in perspective. I had convinced myself that if I didn't contribute above and beyond the required need, everything would fall apart. I was constantly challenging those around me to work more and go further. I had become overly zealous and a bit delusional. No one around me was willing to intervene. There were shifts going past 25 and 26 hours straight. In the meantime, home was becoming a place to just sleep and eat. I was a zombie. I remember during the height of that time the VP calling me and saying, "did you really work 97 hours last week?" I remember my reply like yesterday. I said, "Of course I did, you don't want those automotive plants shut down, do you?" He never called back and questioned my hours again. Not that I am a cowboy, but that is the way it is sometimes. People want you to get the job done at any cost, even if it is to the detriment of you or your family. Which tells me that you must be the one in the driver's seat when it comes to your family. Even good people will watch you destroy your life in the name of "faith in you". Of course, they will honor your achievements and praise you along. But sometimes you just need a good reminder of the truth. But even then, if someone comes to you in that delusion, you may decide not to listen and wake up to the facts they are presenting you with.

I finally woke myself up. I don't really know how either. Because I really tried hard to make the necessary adjustments in my home to still manage some normalcy. I gave up hours of sleep every night or day to just have a little bit more time with my wife and kids. I remember the day I considered changing jobs because the thought occurred to me that I could not continue to do this to myself or my family. Our standard shift was twelve hours per day at 5-6 days per week. It was not uncommon for employees to work 60-72 hours per week, even though I was exceeding that. I wrote down what it would look like in three different scenarios based on five day workweeks. Five 24 hour days equal 6,240 hours for 52 calendar weeks. I divided my time between work, sleep, and actual waking time at home and provided the gains as well.

1. **24-hour day – 12 @ work | 6 @ sleep | 6 @ home**
   I. Annual time at home = 3,120 hours
   II. Annual time at work = 3,120 hours
   III. Result - no gain, current situation
2. **24-hour day – 10 @ work | 7 @ sleep | 7 @ home**
   I. Annual time at home = 3,640 hours
   II. Annual time at work = 2,600 hours
   III. Result - + 520 hours at home gained (21 days)
   IV. Result - + 3 weeks, better home, better sleep
3. **24-hour day – 8 @ work | 8 @ sleep | 8 @ home**
   I. Annual time at home = 4,160 hours
   II. Annual time at work = 2,080 hours
   III. Result - + 1,040 hours at home gained (43 days)
   IV. Result - + 6 weeks, best home, best sleep

I sat down and did this math to find out the best option for what I wanted for my family and my own life. I realized that if I could give up my ego and take a job with less hours, it would be the most productive choice. Gaining six more weeks a year helped me to realize this was an easy choice in considering what I had to do. I spoke with my wife and we decided to make a change. It was just a matter of time before the 8-hour job was a reality. Her encouragement in that situation helped me to put things in perspective and see what was important again in life. If you find yourself reading this and you feel guilty, don't. There is time to change. If you led that lifestyle, I encourage you to do everything you can to make those relationships right, now. I know men can lose themselves in their work, I did. And I know that my own realization and the encouragement of my wife pulled me out of it. And honestly, as a father, you will have your own opportunities to speak truth into the lives of your children. It may not always be received, but don't let them waste precious years chasing dreams that aren't their own. Projects are always going to be there, deadlines will never go away, and endless ladder climbing will only take you farther away from what is most important in life.

Nurture

I remember lying on the grass at the park as a six-year-old boy looking up at clouds and imagining what they were. My imagination was in full swing. If I'm not careful, I can do that today. I have always been a bit of a day dreamer. So, obviously one of my children picked up this same trait. She still loves to daydream. And I think there was always a negative stigma for kids who daydream, but I really have found it to be a good thing. My daydreaming has produced some of my best ideas, especially from an engineering design perspective. I think her passion was born from daydreaming too. She has always loved to climb. Self admittedly, she got that form me too. From the time she was crawling, she would make her way to the top of any chairs, tables, or counters in mere seconds. None of my children have come close to the effort this child would exert to climb. You don't want to see your children get hurt, so the nurturing side of you is trying to encourage them to stop certain behaviors. She had fallen off various pieces of furniture multiple times. She had this knot on her forehead that I wasn't sure would ever go away. She was like a bug drawn to the light when it came to heights. We would constantly remind her to not climb things. Finally, at the height of the story, pun intended, it all came crashing down.

My wife and I were home down the street with our newborn twins and our wonderful little climber went to the park with her grandparents. Then we received a call that she had fallen. Not knowing when we got there that it was going to be as severe as it was. It was sold as a sprain… Only upon arrival did we hear the blood curdling screams and saw her on the ground. There was a six-feet tall cement wall at the park, and she made the decision to take a running leap from it as she had seen another kid do. The resulted broken leg almost ended in a complete compound fracture. She had the imprints of the bone marrow on her skin below her knee. In that moment, I was concerned, but also very frustrated, because everything I had ever worked to teach her seemed to not matter. And I know she was just being a kid. Kids have imaginations and they don't always weigh out the consequences of their decisions. So, I picked her up and took her to the emergency room, and to make matters worse, the nurse asked me thought this could have happened any "other way". I know that it was standard protocol, but after what I have been through with my her for the past 7 years, it was the icing on my frustration delight. Even though I didn't cause it, I did really want to spank her when it happened, but I knew that wouldn't solve anything. Facts. I sat there with her in all her pain and tried to comfort her the best I could. Eventually after we got home and got her settled, we had our first conversation about the event. She knew I was disappointed with the decision she made, but I didn't have to tell her. I just reaffirmed my love for her, and we joked about how after this we would find something taller to jump from. She told me that her climbing days were over and that she had no intentions of doing that again. She had learned the lesson the hard way. The experience literally broke her. It was not the way I wanted her to learn the lesson. You never want your children to experience pain. You do everything in your power to help them see the truth. But in this case, life taught her this lesson. And to this day, she may climb some things at times, but never to put herself in risk of injury. So, your encouragement may feel like at times it is falling on deaf ears, but I can assure you, that if you continue nurturing them and loving them even when they make mistakes they will learn what they need to do naturally and they will learn to trust you more.

Promote

Far be it from a father to hold his children back from becoming the best versions of themselves. My kids always loved the movie Matilda. Danny DeVito played a horrible father in that movie. Little Matilda was a very gifted young lady who faced constant adversity. If you want to know what it looks like to hold your children back as a father, I highly recommend this movie. There were many times when Matilda was doing something to educate herself or push her limits and her father would scream at her to come watch TV like the rest of the family. She had no room for exploration, she had no role model for character, and she had no hope for her future. It was quite a sad story regarding the talent she had. For her to find her way, she needed the help of her teacher, Ms. Honey. She helped her to develop an understanding of herself and her abilities. I like to reference the movie to my children when I see them doing something productive or that is extraordinary these days, like reading a book. Calling them Matilda in that moment always makes them smile. They know I get it. They know I notice what they are doing, and I am pleased. However, I want to not only notice what they are doing, but also push them to do their best in every situation. Leave nothing on the table. Make every lick count. I want them to learn to self-identify their talents and abilities and hold themselves to a standard that they will be proud of, not just me. I want that to exist long after I am gone. It will not stand the test of time if it is done at the will of my demands.

With every good promotion at work, there is some attribute shown by an employee that propels them to the next level. Most of the time, we gladly accept promotions. Unless they are to our detriment. Some positions may be loathed or not desirable. But, if it is desirable, it can be viewed as a great opportunity to excel. Often a person will feel the need to be qualified and accepted to take on new responsibilities. Your children are the same way. They long for promotion. They want to take themselves to the next level with you. Every time they are given an opportunity to showcase their talents and abilities, watch out and watch them shine. You must be on the lookout for those opportunities to promote them. Every step along the way is to build trust and respect and it shared between both of you. Encouragement in the form of promotion is the way every relationship grows. Just like setting aside time for your children as mentioned earlier to work on a project together, you can set apart time and situations that allow them to prove they are worthy of more freedom or whatever they are seeking. Maybe it is a later curfew or to drive the car. You should put in the time, even if it cuts into your plans.

When you push your children's failures in their face or tell them they aren't qualified, what you are really doing is rejecting them. At least that is the way it feels to them. Those statements or actions are extremely hard to overcome, and you can only take so many. Criticality is a very real thing that many children face every day. You may not see the signs of physical abuse on a child, but if you could see their brain, it would be quite tattered and worn. A father who finds no promotional encouragement for his children is typically only reenacting what he experienced. But the good news is that the cycle can be broken. What it takes is being honest with yourself. You must consider yourself in the same situation. It is really the only way to find clarity of mind. Think back to when your child was learning to walk, you would never tell them that they can't do it. No, you try everything to get them to take those first steps and you make sure you catch them if they are falling. Why? Because you care for them. You don't want to see any harm come to them. And that is still your motivation today. A father cannot afford to lose that caring assurance that allows your child to know someone in this world believes in them and does not see them as a failure.

Vision

The coercion that exists in the world is very real. People will persuade or force your children into situations that will not be towards their benefit. Sometimes physically, sometimes by strategy. By now, as fathers we have realized one universal truth – if it is too good to be true, it probably is. Again, I don't want to paint the entire world as bad. You should provide insight and vision to your child through nonstop encouragement. You must help them paint their own picture of what they are to become. But I want you to consider what is waiting for children the day they graduate high school if they see college as an option. In some cases, even earlier because some kids start while they are in high school. When they consider the cost, normally they go and talk to a course advisor first to understand the workload and time cost. Afterwards, the advisor directs them to speak with another advisor about financial aid cost. So, now they have a good idea of the total time and financial costs associated with the pursuit of a college education. Many children don't receive scholarships, tuition payments, or have college savings plans to inherit from their families. So, the options to attend are simple; *A. they don't attend, B. their parents pay, C. they pay.*

With **Option A**; I am ok with that idea, because our society has forced people and especially kids into believing college is necessary for success. Every person does not aspire to become a genetic scientist or a biochemical engineer. But if they want to pursue careers in public service or skilled trades, there are plenty of opportunities for more specific trainings and education that don't always involve college.

Option B is on you. If you want to take on thousands of dollars of debt through financial aid or just pay the loan or make cash payments that is totally up to you. If you set aside money for your children's future, you did a great job. But I think the worst scenario is that you pay for a degree that allows your child to major in a field that has no application or implication today. I have always encouraged my children to think about their future and reminded them that one day they would need to decide if college was for them and what they wanted to do. With each child, those things have changed many, many times. But my resounding message to them is that if they wanted to pursue being a Laffy Taffy taste tester, they should pursue a degree that allows them to do that, and in the process begin speaking with an employer, preferably Laffy Taffy, but I would also suggest their competitors, Airheads. They always got a good laugh out of that and it helped them to have a real understanding of how planning works. Your job is to equip them with the possibilities for their future and help them to not wander aimlessly.

My personal choice has been **Option C**. I have worked very hard to encourage my children to start thinking about their future very early. I want them to profess what they believe they have passion for and then work towards those things. The good and bad news is that they do it, but often, they change. But in the exercise of it and when you encourage them with the greater purpose, they understand the mechanics. And in that understanding of what it takes to pursue a degree and future occupation, I encouraged them to understand the financial cost. Just because they will be paying for their own college doesn't mean I haven't prepared for that. I am not telling you to abandon them.. I made it clear for my children, there are no handouts and there will be no government financial aid loans. So, if four years must move to six to be sure they start out their working careers debt free, so be it. I do not want myself or my children to be put under the financial pressure of loans. Loans with interest. For education. Sounds silly, but the facts are we have a problem here in America with debt. Hard to believe right? If you don't have something or you want something, go get a loan, right? No, not in our house. No, not for my children.

The agreement made between my oldest daughter and I was that she would pay for her own college and work full time. And that is what she does. 3.5 GPA and above get her full reimbursement from the bank of Dad. Incentives to work hard keep commitment intact. I believe in reciprocal commitments. I have heard far too many horror stories of parents paying thousands of dollars for education, only to have the child drop out or lose the necessary focus to see it through. I don't want to be that dad, and neither should you. I'm sorry if this was you. And I know this is again common across America. But the worst thing is when the child doesn't know any better and is innocent prey to the college financial advisors, who may not have the child's best interest at hand.

A few years ago, I had a conversation with a young man in his early twenties who was stacking parts in a manufacturing plant. It was disheartening to hear that he was 24 years old, making $11 per hour and had over $100,000 in student loans. His education was for high performance diesel mechanics, but the problem was that the degree was in such a specialized, overcrowded field, he could not get a job. So, his only option was to work there and hope something came up, but you could tell he had lost hope. I think his monthly payment for loans only left him with $125 each month to live on. And the saddest thing of all, is there is no default for these kids. I know this is probably just the tip of the iceberg for most American students, but at 24, life is not supposed to be this way. Provide vision for the future for your children. One day, they will work and face the same situations you do in their career choices. You just want to be sure they aren't doing it from a position of financial turmoil.

My family and I are debt free! Thanks to our hard work and Dave Ramsey. One of the greatest things you can provide for your children is a vision of what it means to be debt free and experience financial freedom. I am grateful that we realized that as a family. It taught me and my family a valuable lesson in commitment, sacrifice, and hard work. We had spent years behind the eight ball. Living paycheck to paycheck, buying things we didn't need. Trying to impress people we didn't really know. Maintaining a lifestyle that wasn't conducive for a healthy family environment. Arguing about bills and the stress that comes along with being broke. Those things never provide proper vision and are not encouraging when you inform your children they can't do certain things in life because you don't have the money. See this big fancy truck honey, daddy is driving that now so you can't go to college, just doesn't feel right. Although we may not say that to our children, we are living examples providing them a glimpse into the future we are creating for them.

When we finally got sick and tired of being sick and tired, we sat down and planned to change our lives forever. We sold everything we had, paid off all our debts, and changed the game. We stopped depending on credit cards and loans. We got a bit extreme. And to be honest with you, the real motivation was finally realizing that if we didn't stop this behavior, we were guaranteeing a very difficult future for our children. This poverty mentality had to die. It would no longer be accepted or have the opportunity to be passed down to my children. While we did use most of the baby steps and direction provided by Dave Ramsey, it was one item that helped us stay on course as a family. It was "The Ugly Book." Ah, the Ugly Book. I am sure you've heard of it, right? Probably not, but I do have the only Dave Ramsey autographed version in existence on my bookshelf at home. No, he is not the author. It was our family who made this book. One night at dinner, we decided to make the Ugly Book. The book was made of construction paper on the spine, and standard copier paper for the body. And boy, was it ugly! We decided, the uglier it was, the better. The fact that it was ugly was completely intentional to serve as a reminder of how ugly debt is and how bad it is for any family's future. Internally it had big numbers written on every page. All the way to 168. We had already completed over six months of paying off debt and now just had 168 days until we were completely debt free. We needed something that would intensify our efforts and keep us focused on the goal together as a family. Every night we would finish dinner and then we would individually write entries as a family on each page how we felt about the day. Not just as a journal or a diary, but as a physical reminder and encouragement to what we committed to on the back of the book. We made very specific rules to keep us on track and achieve our very clear financial goals. They were as follows;

1. **NO dining out - *it is always cheaper to eat at home***
2. **NO online shopping – *support local businesses***
3. **NO impulse buying - *shop with a plan***
4. **NO second car purchase - *only after we were debt free and then cash only***
5. **NO complaining - *only encouragement***

Then at the bottom of that, we had signature lines that signified we all agreed and would hold each other accountable through this commitment as a family. Once signed, we all did our best to keep it on track. We wrote things on the pages like – "today was really hard", "45 days left!", "really wanted to go out for Mother's Day dinner, but I want to be debt free worse!" They were very real entries that captured what it was like to be a family and struggle together and the greatest part was the real encouragement and vision for the future. And I honestly believe without that level of commitment and everyone doing their part we couldn't have done it with the efficiency we did. It held me to a much higher standard because I knew I could no longer let them down. And I am a better father because of it.

Shortly after we crushed our goal, I had an opportunity to meet Dave Ramsey in person. It was an incredible thing to meet the man who encouraged me and my family. I handed him the

"Ugly Book", and he stood there stunned and asked me "What in the world is this?" I told him it was my family's blood, sweat, and tears summarized in a battle for financial freedom. He smiled and told me "Great job!" I couldn't have been happier to receive that great job. I knew that without him, I may not have ever considered the importance of providing vision for the future to my children. Because of him, I am a better man today. I am more responsible and more considerate of our future. And in that example, I want you to know that you are your children's version of Dave Ramsey. You are providing a vision for their future based on the level of encouragement and guidance you provide, whether you realize it or not.

Chapter 11 | Study

Within my working career today, I am given the opportunity to educate and train individuals and companies all around the country to help them learn how to use highly sophisticated equipment for the purpose of manufacturing. The very first question I ask people is "have you read the manual?" What do you think the most common reply is? It is definitely a resounding "no" and it is at least 75% of the time. And this is for equipment for systems that can easily put you over one million dollars cost. When I first stepped into this role, we didn't really offer the type of training we do now. I immediately saw a need to develop this program and move it forward. The industry was pushing for it. I put together a complete training package that I thought would equip people to better understand and troubleshoot their equipment. I pulled some information from our parent organization that had been used up to that point only internally and formed a program to provide comprehensive training in a more concise and effective way. When I combined the two and added what our customers were requesting, it turned in an item that sold itself. At the heart of it, every business wants to make money, but I have found there is real satisfaction in being able to truly help people become their own expert. In a way, it freed me from calls that in the beginning really bogged down and killed my time. Very simple things to understand can sometimes take more time to explain over the phone than just replacing something that may be broken. But, when you dedicate time, energy, and effort to delivering something of value to your customers, you are empowering them and freeing yourself. The unnecessary calls started going away and repeat business for those customers went up. But not just from a service aspect, but with additional sales as well. Because if you help them to create redundancy plans or action plans, they are better prepared in case of an emergency. Proper planning can be applied if you determine the potential for the issues that can emerge. I shared documentation with my customers that cut through the time wasted and created standards in which they could easily navigate and apply. And the best thing about better management is that stress levels go down. Yes, of course the customer may forget or have an accident occur that is out of their control, but you can use those opportunities to know where to really focus your attention. If I find that one error continues to happen, I really emphasize it more in the next trainings. And in doing that, it helps me to listen and apply myself more eagerly to what they need. I don't just skip over it as this person is just dumb or they just can't get it. I really try to make every voice matter.

Being critical can come quite natural for us as men, but it is far better to listen and study to execute change that helps one another. When I consider what it means to be a good trainer, I must work hard to listen and leave them in a better position than when I arrived. If I can't do that; then why am I doing it? People respect you more when you are willing to help them understand rather than just throw a manual at them and say to read it. And surprise, kids are the same way! You don't get to just have them and not help them improve. There is no physical manual for individual details of life, but that is where you and their mom come in. But since I am not a mom, and you most likely are not as well, I will refrain from telling you how to be a living manual as a mom for your children. What I am going to show and explain below are the same examples used previously, reiterated to help your children get the most out of their lives. Not run a perfect life but give it a very good shot.

Individuality

Like I said before, my grand tally for my children is five. I have no plans as of today to increase that number. I think my wife is finally convinced that five is a good healthy number. Please don't encourage her to think any different. Every one of my children are completely wonderful in their own unique way. I do not mean that facetiously either. One has prayed for the economy since she was very little, fought with me about her desire to not wear her glasses, and at times, loved sports more than people. One has been a nerd since she was born, fought with me to wear her glasses, and taught me many lessons in fashion. One has fought with me for her ability to fly from high places, is extremely creative, and has a heart as big as the ocean. The twins are rambunctious, life giving, exhausting, and we are just getting started out good. One of them is extremely demanding, a princess, and requires glamour. One of them is strong willed, speaks like a doctor, and commands attention. In my mind I can see each one in their own light and the special features they provide to life and our family. As a father, may I do everything to allow them to not lose their wonder. When you look into the eyes of your children, you see not only them, but their complete being and all the beautiful experiences you have had with them along the way. Even the tough times are beautiful. A father never has to be convinced how special his children are. It is a known to him. Do everything you can to promote and preserve that individuality.

One of the worst things you can do is compare them or pit them against another sibling, friend, or anyone for that matter. Teaching them to laugh at themselves and accept their shortcomings as part of being a human is far greater than to hold them against an unachievable standard. It is as if you or I stand in front of a one-thousand-foot wall and are screamed at and told to jump over it. You must understand their own unique individuality in terms of the expectations you are placing over their lives. Even against yourself, it can be quite unfair. Our life experiences are far more different, and we may not always take into consideration the full story. The angle of showing them where they performed better than you is always the better angle. Find ways to celebrate their accomplishments and ways that promote them to determine their own future because of their own beliefs, experiences, and understanding of the world. There is a whole chapter dedicated to the views of correction and discipline, but in this case, I am referring you to know your child better, so you can help influence them to be themselves.

Countless musicians and artists tell the stories of how they started out their careers and some honest record label producer basically told them we already have the artist you are attempting to sound like. Many of them took that advice to heart and they quickly found their own voice. And when that happened, success was just around the corner if they could hang on to the journey. And that is the role I am asking you to play in the life of your children. When you see the talent in them that needs to be called forth, be brave enough to speak to them in the truth and help them develop their own voice in this world. I want you to be a master in understanding your child. And in doing that, you must study them, every detail of their life. You need to know what makes them tick, how to hold their attention, and the best way to truly connect with them. There is going to be so many opportunities to parent them, even as you age. It doesn't stop when they move out, the role just changes a bit.

I have four songs that are treasured between myself and each one of my children. The songs are unique and have major significance in our life. Kind of like a wedding song you may share with your wife. I still remember the song my wife and I shared at our wedding and it still feels like yesterday. I remember the same for my children. There seemed to be a moment that was carved out in time just for us to identify it. May I preface this story by saying I am very diverse in my musical taste, but you will notice that our songs are all country songs. I appreciate the honesty and sincerity of country music as I age. Our songs are "Love without end, amen", by George

Strait; "My little girl", by Tim McGraw; "The world", by Brad Paisley; and "One boy, one girl", by Collin Raye; that last one is obviously for my twins. Every time these songs play, I am thrown into the moment. And they serve as a reminder to my children the fact that we have a song and that it's uniquely ours. I mention this also because they are much more than just songs. I have requested to my wife that if I pass before she does to remember that I want only these songs played at my funeral. Maybe a little somber for what I just shared, but I really don't want that day to be about what I did, but how much they meant to me. I take being a father very serious and I don't live considering death not to be a real thing, as I am afraid many of us do. And because of that, I can be assured that they too will take their responsibilities very serious as well.

Eliminate distractions

Hobbies are awesome, just not at the expense of your relationships. It is extremely easy to get things out of balance when we are having fun. I often dream about fishing. Not sure why, but I do. And I enjoy it, but not as much as when I was a kid. Now I am more limited to just take the kids for fun when I do. When I was growing up, my family would probably be viewed as extremists when it came to the importance of fishing and hunting. I am positive looking back on it that there were many years it ranked first in order of priorities, even ahead of family. At Thanksgiving dinner, it was not uncommon for everyone to be in the woods for the day on a hunt. It was like we couldn't get enough. If it wasn't deer season, it was turkey season that kept us in the woods. The fishing trips were all throughout the year as well. I had fun and made some great memories from those times with my grandpa and my uncles. But, as I grew older it didn't seem fun anymore, it felt like a chore. I felt like I was missing out on other things in life. My life didn't feel balanced. I thought about my grandmother who was always at home by herself and it made me sad for her. It didn't feel very considerate. She never said anything to make me think that, but I guess I just realized a change in her demeanor. I think loneliness is real and I think that is what she was feeling.

If you knew your kids were feeling that way about you being away with work or your hobbies, would you notice? I know you need your own things to enjoy. But, just don't forget that when you have a family, you cannot forsake them. Like I mentioned in earlier chapters, I committed myself to my work as an extreme and didn't realize it. I honestly did not see it. I was fortunate to wake up to what I was doing and because I did, my relationships with my children are better for it. But I know that isn't always the case. One of my daughter's friends was over for dinner one night and we were having our normal after dinner conversations and she stopped us right in the middle. She told us that we really didn't understand how blessed we were to be able to sit together and have meaningful conversations. Then she proceeded to tell us how she never spent time like that with her family and that most nights she just stayed in her room and ate something that came from the microwave. Again, I detected the loneliness. She then told me that if her dad wasn't working, he was on the golf course, or on social media all night. It was so sad to hear her express this hidden pain. I told her the best course of action was to pull her dad aside and tell him how she felt. I don't know how things turned out, but it helped me to realize I don't need to take what I have with my family for granted. And I realize that it's not just your hobbies or your work that can distract you, it's also media of any kind. It is almost impossible to go out for dinner these days and not see every table focused on their cell phones rather than the people they are sitting with. You would be hard pressed to find anything different. The distractions are very real. It is so important to recognize when you aren't giving someone your full attention. It is so easy to do. The cell phones are just a portion. I can remember the TV being the same issue when I was a child. I saw parents of my friends so engrained in the TV that their kid could have said, "Hey mom, I am going to set the house on fire", and the response would have been a mindless "ok, if you say so." We cannot afford to take our hands off the steering wheel in life. I know you love your shows and keeping up with what everyone else is doing on social media, but you must focus on the task at hand. I swear those rants and those posts never change. You aren't missing much. Maybe just the fact that someone ate ketchup on their BBQ chips and felt inspired to show you and there five thousand "friends".

Listen

Even if it's true, we've all heard the old statements of "you have two ears and one mouth, so you should listen twice as much as you talk." And, "just because you aren't talking doesn't mean you are listening". In fact, you may be lost in a daydream as the conversation is fading into sounding like Charlie Brown's teacher. I had a manager one time that I tried to model my working career after. He had a rare ability to listen to people. Not just let them talk, but to truly engage them in a way that they felt heard. He wasn't perfect, but he had a real knack for communication with his employees and potential business partners. He was completely intentional in his communication. He taught me several principles to live by when engaged in conversation, whether he meant to or not. I witnessed him turn many situations of business around and in the favor of our company because of his abilities.

I vividly remember as a young man, sitting in a very important meeting with a customer who was not happy with the results that were yielded from a material process study and he began banging his fists on the table in frustration. I wondered if things were going to turn violent at one point. No one had really done anything wrong, but he was displeased that the result for the new material testing did not yield the results he expected. I watched my manager calm him completely by just listening to him with full attention. It was as if I watching a dangerous animal be soothed into submission. After the meeting, I told my manager I was really impressed with how he calmed the customer down. He laughed and told me that sometimes people just need to get their frustrations out and be heard; and you can normally tell how serious it is by how far the veins on their neck are protruding from the skin. He was also letting me know that we shouldn't take every outburst so seriously, but always focus on finding the peace in the situation. I learned so much from him when it came to the art of listening.

There has been nothing more critical to projects in my career than my coworkers giving misinformation about customer visits or just not remembering certain details. One time I remember attending a customer meeting with a colleague and there was a multi-million-dollar project on the line. We were in the initial phases of discussing the expectations. I saw a tremendous opportunity and the feedback from the customer was the same when we offered up a potential solution at the meeting. It wasn't going to be easy, but it wasn't impossible. Upon our return, I realized my colleague had different thoughts when he told our manager it didn't go well and there was no way we could help them with this project. I immediately called him out and said, "what meeting did you attend?". I reminded him that the customer was going to ship parts to us to begin trials and we agreed that we would begin planning for production, if they were successful. Why would we have done that if we didn't believe this project had a chance? It wasn't like we didn't know how to say no. Sometimes, I felt like we were too good at that, but this opportunity looking very favorable. This was the first time in my career I noticed how listening or not listening could cause very severe implications. If I hadn't been there to defend what we told the customer, the project would have died right on those steps where we had the discussion with our manager. But because it didn't, over the next year, that project exceeded over two million dollars. Misinformation or not listening can be completely detrimental to your relationships. People want to know they can depend on you to help them find solutions. But, if you struggle with good listening skills, make sure you can take good notes. We will cover that below as well, don't worry if you didn't listen to that last part.

The main point of this section is for you to understand how important it is to develop the skill to listen with intent and to know the difference between existing, hearing, and listening. And listening doesn't always mean you have to do or fix something. Just the simple acknowledgement is golden when it comes to life. Not that you are trying to add a compliment or show that you disagree, but that by listening, you show that you truly care. As a father, correction is not your only objective. There are times when even you or I do not have the answers. You and I will need to sit with them through the pain. My heart breaks for families with childhood cancer weighing down on them daily. There is a scene from a movie that my wife suggested we see on a weekend getaway one time. I wasn't sure what I was getting myself into by agreeing, but nonetheless, I went along. The movie was called "My sisters' keeper." It was about a young girl who had cancer and her sister was her marrow donor. Her sister who donated the marrow took the parents to court because she didn't feel she had been given the freedom to decide for herself if she even wanted to. But it was a ploy by her big sister, so she could stop struggling with her cancer once and for all. I have never cried so much in my life. I cried until I had a headache. It felt like dehydration from crying, if that is possible. And I know some of you may even be going through very difficult things like this, feeling completely out of control or helpless, but my only advice is to hold on and just be there, listening. In the movie, towards the end of the little girl's life, she sat there in her hospital bed with her family. As she sat there fading, some of them offered up vain solutions on what they read online about holistic approaches and if you just believed you were better, you would be. And I know there are plenty of us who are amped up in the power of faith and in our bodies to heal itself. But this movie pointed to something else. This wasn't about her healing at all. This moment in the movie displayed the stark contrast in our most basic function as human beings, and that was to show compassion to others. It can be quite a disgusting thing when people accuse others that they didn't have enough faith or belief before they pass. I have personally seen it. I don't have answers for why we will so inevitably suffer or have painful experiences in our life, but what I do know, is that they are much easier to make it through when we have people surrounding us who operate from compassion in everything they do. And that is the heart of listening to your children; compassion.

Growth

How can you expect to be good at something, if you don't grow? Leaders are readers, right? I mentioned earlier that many companies and organizations spend millions of dollars every year for you to advance as a leader or improve at some specialized skill. My father inspired me as a young man when he decided at almost forty years old to go back to college and pursue a degree. It was quite unbelievable to see. He had worked the same job for almost twenty years at that point. If that isn't an effort towards growth, I don't know what it is. He worked hard to go to work and school and get an education. He had seniority over many of the people he worked with and had done almost every job in the plant over his tenure. But then the announcement came that there was going to be a layoff and then the plant was going to cease production. My father had moved into his new department because of the education he pursued. He was the newest team member. This department was going to retain only two of the fourteen employees in this group to maintain the premises and equipment during the indefinite shutdown. The plant employed over 400 people, and now the plan was to only keep three. He was one of the three. His seniority would not have kept him in that position alone, but because he pursued his education, he was now in the department that kept the two and he was now in. How does that happen? I call it a miracle, not sure what you call it. What are the chances? I believe in Divine intervention and provision because I have seen it too many times, not because I read it in a book. This opportunity happened in the name of growth. His employer did not push him into this position, something simply sparked within him that this was important and must be pursued.

To become good at almost anything, you must study and set yourself up for growth. Why is it that we think we have it all together when it comes to parenting? Maybe you are good at it. But I think it's not that thinking that makes you approach it that way. It is just the fact that you haven't considered how you can become a better father. I really believe that for you. Because I have seen it in me as well. I have had many times that I felt like I really had myself together as a dad, but reality hit me in the face. I suggest taking part in conferences and courses that help you to approach better parenting angles. Read books not just through the lens of what the topic is, but in a way that these things you are learning may apply to your special relationships. You won't always find the right answer fast, but if you pursue what you need to know, it will show up. There are some amazing organizations out there that can help you to become the best version of yourself as a father. But you must be on the lookout for them. I would much rather know that I am not just sitting on my hands thinking I have it all together than to lose out on helping my child see that I am really trying to be the best I can be. Sometimes, insight like that can help you to ask the right questions. There has been a thirty percent increase in suicides over the past twenty years. Can you honestly spot the symptoms in your child today, if you were asked to? Many fathers are shocked everyday with the tragic news of losing their son or daughter to suicide. Many of them feel like they should have known or could have done more. I want you to be proactive in their life and prepared to have the toughest of the tough conversations. Study and grow into the father that they need. You will not be guaranteed success, but you will know that you always did your best.

Take notes

This part is super critical for what we will discuss in the next chapter. I need you to start today writing or typing notes in a journal entry titled under your child's name on your phone or in a notebook. It is important to note their successes, failures, qualities, experiences, and goals. And it is important to note your insight for their life and how you can address them. Write something down and you are more likely to remember it over just taking mental notes. So, by doing this, your memory will stay fresh when it comes to what is going on individually in the life of your child or children. Writing notes not only keeps the items on your mind, it allows you to focus on what is important. And that is developing a deeper, more meaningful relationship. When you are in the mode of observance toward them, you can't help but focus on them. Now they will have your attention, and they will notice. You don't have to write down every mistake either, this isn't about micromanagement. Just jot down what matters. The intention of taking these notes will come out shortly. In my phone under the notes section, I have all their names filed under their own folder. When something happens that I deem noteworthy, I enter it into the file. It is a piece of cake to do, if I am intentional. So, when you take notes, you are making sure you don't forget anything, and you are reminding yourself what to focus on, and most importantly, you are retaining very valuable information for the long term.

Take chances on what you record. Make assumptions about what you are writing down. Dig deeper into the thoughts you have and don't just be a stenographer; you know, the person who is constantly typing when people talk in a court room. There must be a real purpose behind what you are recording as notes. For example, if you write something about how they performed during a game, don't just write "I watched you at your game." That's just creepy. Write something like "At your game, I noticed your crossover is really improving; broken ankles everywhere!" Record notes in a way that is relevant for them and show them the details of the experience. You are not doing this to check off a list. I want you to do it with the mindset of a dad who loves his children and is looking for every way to show it. If your children are older, I know your opportunities are more limited. But every time you talk to them or find out something that is going on in their life, take the time to write it down and make it important when you do. Again, this part is super critical for what we discuss in the next chapter. Do it! You can do it!

Chapter 12 | Write

So, at this point we have reviewed the fundamentals of fatherhood, not really topic by topic, but regarding most major themes. I have shared my thoughts and many of my very personal stories and insights. When the idea I am about to share with you first came to me, it didn't feel like an idea at all. It was almost as if someone spoke it in my mind directly. I am completely aware of what I am saying. And I am completely aware of the fact that we have a subconscious working in the background of our mind. But when this happened to me, it was more like someone giving me directions on something, not like I was inspired by a thought or statement, not because I was brainstorming, and not because I am just so smart. I wasn't even looking for this type of instruction. If you would have asked me, I would have said I am a pretty good father, or at least try to be. When the idea came, I was attending a two-day conference in Dallas and the speakers were just talking about commercial ideas regarding finances, growth, and strategy. There were absolutely no discussions about family or anything considerably frilly for business topics. As I was listening to a speaker talk about his company growing to one of the largest in his state for his specific industry, it was as if everything around me got really quiet, and I heard in my mind this statement, "I want you to start writing letters to your children." I was startled at the thought of it. I immediately took out my phone and wrote in the Notes app on my phone. Then it was like the details began to be downloaded in my mind. There were very specific items like, your children are to receive the letters on the date of their births each month. So, if one of their birthdays is on June 8th, they are to receive a letter on the 8th of every month. In my original note I recorded, it says the content is to be completely selfless and that they need to be made aware that you are here and listening. The content is also to be more than just saying they are awesome; you must talk about the hard-hitting items too. If their grades are down because they are struggling to find balance in something new, help them to remember their priorities. I had never heard of any idea like this or anyone doing it and it completely blew my mind. After the conference, I called my wife and told her about the incident. I think the notion left her in awe as well. It was so simple, but so profound. I couldn't wait to start, it literally felt like Christmas morning to me. I could not wait to get home and begin. But then all the thoughts began to enter my mind. This was something completely new to my role as a father. Nobody tells you that you need to write letters every month to your children for the rest of their lives, but when you truly think about the impact of having someone else, especially your father, speaking life into everything you do, it is supremely spectacular. I considered that my kids may not be open to letters, because we live in such a digital world and that they may not really take them serious or even worse, see them as cheesy. I considered my oldest who had never received a letter from me and if she would think it odd. I really didn't even know how to start the letter, the more and more I thought about it. Then I had the funniest thought; am I about to die? I really thought that. But over the years I have really considered how to avoid doing things I regret and what does a life look like to live it without regrets. So often, we chase the wind and pursue things that will not stand the test of time. I have said it already in the book, but I will say it again. I do not want to lay on my deathbed and carry regrets. I want to know that in everything I have put my hand to, I truly did my best. But even more so, I believe with my whole heart the Biblical scripture Proverbs 3:5-6, which says "Trust in the Lord with all of your heart and lean not on your own understanding, but in all your ways, acknowledge Him and He will make your paths straight." That type of living really takes a ton of pressure off my life. But regrets are a horrible part of life and they can haunt you throughout your life if you let them. Even if you have regrets about your relationships with anyone, you can change them with one decision, today. Forgiveness is how we make a mend with ourselves first. If you can't start the conversation with yourself today, you never will. And if you can't forgive yourself, it is impossible to even think you can receive forgiveness from others. Even if you try to seek forgiveness from your children or in other relationships, it is not guaranteed that the other party is even willing to accept. Which tells me that the responsibility is always on us to make the best of our lives by making sure we make the most of every moment.

I really despise the word "challenge", I think it is almost as overused as the word "leadership." So, rather than challenge you to write letters, I wanted to inspire you to make the changes necessary, give you the insight, and allow you to see for yourself the importance. Maybe you are asking yourself if this applies to me as an older father? And my answer is yes! When I first began writing the letters to my children, I kept it extremely private. Only between me and my children, and of course my wife. Nobody knew that I was doing this. Then one day when I was at a customer site, I met a gentleman there who had five children, just like me. I saw his eyes light up when he began to talk about them. Man, it was really inspiring to see how much he loved talking about his children. And yet sadly, it seemed a bit depressing. Not because of his apparent joy, but because I realized this wasn't happening enough in many of the conversations we have as men. I felt like I was speaking to myself, regarding how much I love my children. He was a little older than me, and most of his children had already moved out and began their families. I believe his oldest was almost thirty. He shared with me that he and his sons had just spent the weekend at a football game and how it was one of their big family traditions. At that moment, I felt as if I heard that same voice that gave me instruction say, "its ok to share what you do with him." It was really against my better judgment at that point. What I was doing with my children was considered sacred to me and I didn't want to share it with anyone. It was just our secret. But again, I listened to that small still voice. I began to tell Royce my secret. He sat there across the table from me with his eyes filling up with tears. He told me had just recently lost his father. I told him I was sorry for making him cry, but he assured me it wasn't my fault, he just said lately he realized how much he missed him and how he didn't want his relationships to slip through his fingers. He really appreciated what I shared with him and told me he was going to start doing the same thing.

Well, a few months went on and I saw Royce again in person and we spoke again like old friends. He told me his family was doing well and we exchanged a few stories. Then I hit him with the big question that had been on my mind, "Have you started writing your letters?" He hung his head and told me that he hadn't. I asked him why. And his response was that he felt like his children were too old now and that he couldn't really offer them any correction or do the fatherly stuff he had been accustomed to doing. At that moment, I understood what he was saying. But that still small voice showed up again and said, "it is not supposed to be this way." I felt compassion for what Royce said, but it didn't mean I wouldn't respond. I said "Royce, being a father is so much more than just offering correction. It means that somebody in this world knows you, has your back no matter what, and will never leave you or forsake you, even if they aren't physically here." Your words and actions live on through your children, whether you realize it or not. When they leave your house, that doesn't have to stop. He understood what I was saying. But then my Helper, my still small voice prompted me to say this – "Royce, how would you feel today to receive a letter from your father?" The tears were real for both of us at that point. It was an aha moment for both of us. I knew Royce was special, I just didn't realize how much. And I knew I had this unrelenting reason for sharing my secret with him. He began telling me how the letters meant more to him than I understood. They were extremely personal. He told me something he had never told anyone else. He said that when he was in the Army, his friends would pay him to write letters to their girlfriends back home. He said he wrote hundreds of them during that time. My jaw hit the floor. I am speaking to a man that had spent most of his time writing letters for his friends because they felt like it was hard to express how they felt or just felt inadequate with their words. If anyone could ever understand what I was trying to do here, it was Royce. This was the second reason why I realized it wasn't just enough to share the letters with others to help them with their relationships, there had to be real thoughts and effort applied to what it meant to open up and reveal yourself as a father.

Application

By now, you have surely surmised the intent of the book. Sometimes just having a manual is not enough to just understand a product. Like I explained earlier with my functions of training, I normally spend the first day on theory and covering a manual of sorts. Then the second day, we spend in the shop getting our hands dirty and applying what we've learned. Head knowledge is just that, but when you put feet on what you understand, great things can happen. One of my greatest joys in my career has been to help people understand very complex things in the simplest manner. And when those things you share are understood, there is an appreciation that cannot be faked. It is completely empowering and if we don't watch out for the opportunities, we can so easily miss out. Just today as I was talking with my son about losing his baby teeth, I was reminded of how challenging it can be at times to explain such simple concepts. We were talking about him starting kindergarten and he started to get upset and told me how he did not want to lose his baby teeth. He cried and said he didn't want to look like an old grandpa. I explained to him that we will have two sets of teeth over our life and that there are already new big teeth like mine waiting to take the place of the ones we lose. I showed him my teeth and he said they were too big for his mouth. Kids are honest and funny again. But in just that few minutes of conversation, you realize talking about things in a way that helps others to understand really is for the greater good of humanity, if we just take the time. Who knows, he may have carried quite a heavy amount of fear about losing his teeth, had we not had that conversation. But now, he has a better understanding and believes for the best.

When you begin to write these letters to your children, I want you to remember that you will get better in time. Don't be too hard on yourself if they aren't perfect. Write them as if you are telling your younger self what you have learned in life and how to properly navigate the pitfalls and hurdles that came your way. I can't convince you of your passions or convictions because they are yours. We all have our own individual life experiences that shape who we are. But as a father speaking to another father, I just ask that you operate in the guidelines I have written down for you. The heart of a good father is selfless and has the best of intentions for his children. I don't want you to write letters that infer guilt, condemnation, or feelings of shame upon your children. I have two things I really struggle with when I detect it in other people. Arrogance and imposed guilt. And I believe I am not alone in that. Suppose you are a very successful person. The worst way to convey to your children to pursue greatness is by comparing them to yourself and your accolades. Your children will always respect humility more. Most normal people do. Of course, there are megalomaniacs and narcissists among us, but children typically don't fall into that category. It is a bit of a learned or promoted behavior. Imposed or forced guilt is horrible. You know those people, right? The ones that you can never please. I am sure when Michelangelo painted the ceiling of the Sistine Chapel, one of them said to him, "couldn't you have finished it quicker?" To teach your kids not to be focused on being people pleasers, you must remember it starts with you. The heart of both of those attributes people show is that whatever you do, you will never meet their standard or expectations. A father can teach their children acceptance, and that is all people ever really want. Just the action of writing to them will change you as a father. You will begin to take the relationship more seriously. The wisdom will begin to grow, and you will see patterns come more into the light as you grow the relationships. And in them, they learn that they have more than a friend. They have a father who cares.

In the application of writing them a letter, you need to also consider how you deliver the letter, and the mechanics of how this works in more detail. Not only do I write the letter, I am very specific about how they receive it. I try hard to get it to them on the day of their birth, each month, but if I am off a day or two, they are ok with that. But don't get outside of that, because I promise you, they will notice. When I first started writing the letters, they were kind of like "oh, cool, thanks." But it slowly morphed into, "where's my letter dad?"; if it was even one day late. I think they live for those letters now. When I give them their letters it is always in a very specific way. I normally sit in my chair in my bedroom and they sit across from me on the edge of my bed. When they open the letter, I make sure we are eye to eye across from each other. Child psychologists have proven many times over it is not a great idea to speak down to your children. It is overly intimidating, and you should keep that in mind any time you communicate with them. I have even considered that with my wife, as I tower over her. But she is not above snatching me down to her size, and I realize that. So, it's not truly a fair assessment. But nonetheless, with your children, don't forget that how you position yourself to them matters. It is also important to do it in person, if you can't do it in person, at least over the phone in real time or video chat. I don't want you to create lag or lose impact in the moment. If you can only mail the letters, make sure you get them on the phone before they read it. After they have opened the letter, I ask them to read it to me aloud and once they have finished, I ask them to tell what they think. I then listen and let them talk. I want to know what they are thinking. Normally, emotions are involved somewhere along the way, from both of us. These are very intimate moments we share. I give them a little more input as they explain how they feel or what they think, but not too much. I want my letter to really carry the weight of what I had to say as a summary for the month. Again, another reason why it is so important to take good notes and study them. It all comes out here. I normally gather about four or five main comments or thoughts for the letter. I make it around one page long each time. My initial letter was three pages to each one of them because it was the introductory letter and I felt that I really needed to explain my intentions. And again, it was quite alarming how I felt during that first letter. I just kept feeling like I am going to die soon. I had to really shake that thought and focus on the bigger picture here. I think I felt that way because we just don't always operate so direct and deep. But it has proven to be well worth it. I have seen a real change in the relationships with my children. Every time we sit down to do the letters, it feels brand new. It has become expected. I have started something that I don't think can be stopped, and that is my hope for you.

When I first approached the girls about writing a book about the letters, they were immediately all for it. The feedback they gave me is that the letters were life changing and they believed there was a real need out there for fathers to step up their game. Because they were seeing the results firsthand from the kids who didn't have fathers in their life they knew personally. They obviously don't know what that is like, but being in school, it is easy for them to get the idea. But I told them I really wanted to have something that could impact others in the same way this has impacted us. But it wasn't enough to just say to you – "write some letters and your relationships will automatically get better". That could be dangerous in the hands of someone who really didn't understand the responsibility and reason for doing it. If you want to write the letters and do them the same way I do, I back you one million percent. But if your motives or heart isn't right, I would ask you to refrain until you can get it right. You can't use them as a way of getting back at your ex-wife, to keep bringing up old wounds, or even to criticize your kids. I cannot say that enough! That would be the most distasteful and despicable thing you could do. The application must be selfless. It must be genuine. And it must be from the heart of a good father.

Get to work!

Start today! Don't wait! Get it done! Maybe up until this point you feel like a failure, but I am encouraging you to get over the pity party and see what truly matters. All your imperfections, failures, and faults can be wiped away with a new future. Build a future of wonder with your children. One in which they never have to question if they are loved. One where they know that they are never alone. That no matter what cost, what effort, what mistake, or what decision, you are always there, always in their corner. Never giving up on them. Fighting for them. Even willing to die for them if necessary. Rarely are we loved in life this way, what a great honor and privilege a father has when he can show his children his allegiance and belief in them, not by just word, but in every deed. No man ever died with regrets for loving his children. He took that joy with him to the grave. You have no time to waste when it comes to your children. Make peace with your past if it is holding you back from the future you and your children deserve. Be honest and real. Be encouraged that today can be a new day. Be mindful that perfection is not required in fatherhood, but the real need is in your effort and commitment.

In closing for the book, I am reminded of my wife and her wonderful personality. She has stood by my side throughout every decision we've ever made together. Her relentless love for me and my children is where most of my inspiration can flow from. In her imperfectly perfect way of being a mother and wife, I can pen my heart's desire for you. She lost her father when she was only five years old. I cannot imagine what that must have felt like. I know the pain is real. We have been to her fathers' grave site several times and each time I can see her trying to collect the very few memories she has of him as a little child. I know she valued that relationship and the short time she had with him with the utmost respect. I've heard stories of his sense of humor and l although I never met him, I can see it in her. I've not always treated my wife the best, as I know some men can admit today. But I am always keeping in mind that I must do better and always strive to do my best. Especially because I know my children are watching how I treat their mother. And don't forget that if you are divorced, because that woman is still their mother, and they will remember how you treated her as well. Always be the better person.

When my wife and I first started dating, I knew she didn't grow up with a dad. It hurt my heart to know that. She didn't even have a stepdad. The closest thing she knew to having a father figure was her brothers, but that is a stretch. One day when we were going through pictures, she showed me a photo of her and her dad when she was in his lap giving him the biggest hug. The picture was taken about a year before he passed. Because I knew I loved her early in our dating, I took that picture and went and had it blown up to an 8" x 10" and put in the most beautiful frame I could find. I gave it to her on her birthday. I think that was the day I truly won her heart. I pondered something more today as I wrote this story. I realized that without her in my life, I might have been with someone else who would have never allowed me to discover what it means to be my own version of a father. And I hope that as you apply these measures in your life that your significant other will inspire and encourage you in the same ways my wife has. Your wife can bring out the best in you as a father if you work together. It was really her who helped me to grow the idea to something even bigger by suggesting that we scan every letter and make a digital copy for the purposes of passing it down in a book to them from year to year. I was, as most men are, focused on the here and now, and she helped me to see the greater future value in handing it down the line. Just goes to show you, we still have a lot to learn.

Chapter 13 | Results

For all the fathers who've read this. Whether in prison, whether divorced, whether not biological, whether deployed, whether on assignment, whether struggling, whether broken, or whether home, I wrote this book for you. I want to give you insights that help you to find your way. I do not expect perfection, and neither should you. You make up 50 % of the person who calls you dad whether they like it or not. In writing these letters, I want you to remember that the purpose is not to be braggadocios or think yourself to be your child's version of a god. Your role is to father. And that is all that it is. We have covered the many facets throughout to enable you to understand that role and how to apply it. May you seek better relationships and long-lasting memories. Your results may not be immediate, or in some cases they may never come. But, know this, they will not be done in vain. You will never carry doubt or regrets as a father if you can connect with them in the deeper way I have shared. I know it because I have experienced the results. I am going to share below three different individual letters I wrote to my children and then also their three interpretations of what the letters mean to them.

Before you begin to read the summarization of this book, I would like to leave you with one lasting thought. Years ago, my wife and I had our genetics testing done to find out our genetic makeup and learn more about our origins. Our motivation was to know where we came from to get an idea about our past. We found out a few very interesting insights about our past, but really nothing more than just geographical information and who our brand new family relatives were. However, another interesting thing we found is that the company would offer your health insights for certain genetic markers that have been found for certain diseases or conditions. One of the genetic markers found for me signaled that I carried a gene that was often found for late onset Alzheimer's disease. You have a choice in these tests of whether or not you want to know. I opted to find out, obviously in hope that if I did have something like this, I could be proactive for the future. Nonetheless, it wasn't extremely exciting news to me. I have personally seen the disease and it is very difficult to watch people lose their memories and sense of self. It is painful and gut wrenching to see them reach out for people who aren't there or not even recognize the face of their children. And from that thought, I leave you with this. If this proves to ever be part of my future, I have full confidence that my children will always have something to hold onto with the letters if I were to ever forget their face or if my time was cut short. Don't forget that we are not promised tomorrow.

Below are the examples of the individual letters I write to my children. I have complete permission to share, so don't worry. After those letters, you will find summaries. Those summaries are written by my daughters, as they all thought it would be important to add to supplement the book. Please enjoy.

Letter 1

Happy Birthday! Today is the most special day of the year for me and your mom! Eleven years ago, we had a very special, little, baby girl. She had big brown eyes and a cute little button nose. You have brought so much joy to our life, and I am so glad you are my daughter. I still remember the first time you said "Dada", the first time you walked, and the first time you climbed a chair and fell off... ahh, memories. It is hard to believe you are eleven years old. Time really flies when you are having fun.

Sometimes, I look at you and wonder what kind of woman and mother you are going to be when you grow up. But not because I want to rush it and get you out of the house fast, but because I know you have a lot of your mom's qualities. And I know your future husband, kids, and family are going to be blessed because of that. You are a hard worker, you never complain when we need you to do something, you always have a good attitude, and you are always willing to serve others. Your grandfather has always said that God has a special plan for that little girl. And I agree.

Love, Daddy

Letter 2

You are extremely talented, dedicated, and passionate with everything you do. The level of commitment you display when you start something is incredible. And not just that, but your ability to finish what you start is going to separate you from everyone else in the future. You've inherited my intense drive to start something and your mom's ability to finish it. That makes me happy. You are the complete package. I only expect great things from you!

This letter is primarily focused on one thing - YOU believing in yourself. I want you to step your game up! Confidence is the name of the game. Don't make the mistake of comparing yourself to others. God has a very specific plan for your life. Having confidence does not mean that you are not humble. It does not mean you are arrogant. You come from a family of late bloomers when it comes to confidence. I am in my thirties and just now feel confident. At your age, I mumbled a lot, had poor posture, walked with my head down, didn't believe in myself, and often cried if other people received compliments and I didn't. I was very insecure. You are already way ahead of me in terms of maturity when I was your age. If one of your friends challenged you to a paint off, you would gladly accept. Why? Because you have full confidence in your ability. Because you know you have put in the countless hours of work. I want you to have that same confidence when

you step on the basketball court and even when you walk. You've got to believe in yourself. If there is something you don't feel confident in, - work on it. Find ways to overcome those doubts and fears. Walk with your head up and shoulders proud. Have your own sense of fashion and style, but not because your ashamed or afraid of how your body appears to you. Embrace who you are, the body God has given you, and have full confidence in your abilities. I fully believe in you and everything you do! Always have, always will.

Love, Daddy

Letter 3

I think you are brave, compassionate, and kindhearted. I see you as a trend setter and a natural born leader. I am never shocked or amazed by your good nature or actions, but I am impressed. To see you work full time, go to school full time, pay for your books and tuition, and stand for something that is truly impactful. I am your dad, but you are your own self. You make your own decisions, you follow your own heart, and you put in all of the hard work. I am truly pleased with the young woman you are becoming. I know you don't need my approval, and you definitely don't have to earn it or ever feel like you have to work to make me happy. I am happy because you are my daughter, and I love you just the way you are. I look forward to seeing what kind of impact you leave on this world.

I really enjoyed our time together and it was a nice "surprise visit", even I knew about it. Your siblings were so happy to see you and spend time with you as well. They could not stop talking about you when you left, and I know they couldn't ask for a better big sister. It is nice to know they will always have you to look up to and that if they ever need someone, you will be there.

September is the time of year when the season begins to change. Summer to fall. While it is very beautiful now, it won't be long, and the leaves will be on the ground. And just like we talked about a few weeks ago, our lives change in the same way. But change is good. Trust the Lord your God with all your heart, lean not on your own understanding, but in all your ways, acknowledge him and he will direct your paths. Love, Daddy

Summary 1

I am not sure how to start this, but I want to say, these letters are worth more than gold to me. They show me how he feels about our accomplishments and maybe even our downfalls. He is fair and he wants us to consider everything we do. It shows us that he is paying attention to the small things. Like the details of band concerts and how certain events went. I understand that most of the time, my dad is busy with the twins, but the letters show us that he is paying attention, even when we think he may not be. I am going to go out and say that I am self-conscious about what I say and wear. And in the letter, he told me that I should be more confident in who I am, and it has allowed me to be more comfortable in my skin. It is literally like Christmas every month! It's like a surprise every time. There are a lot of times when I cry when I read them. It's not just because they are that great; I mean they are, but sometimes when we read them together, I am like, how did he know? Seriously, I could have been questioning myself about something and he would write it down and it would be amazing and exactly what I needed. I love the fact that he asks us to read them to him. When I think of it, it shows me that this is real and that he wrote this. Oh yeah, before I forget, he had to stop writing them in cursive to me because I can't read it at all. Don't complain, I can't help I was born in the 21st century. I love talking about the letters. Because I know I can be open with what I say because he won't be offended about what I say, or I know it won't be outside of a one on one talk. I know he won't go out and be like "guess what she said." And I think that is part of it too. He will keep our conversations private. I don't have to worry about him blabbing to our neighbor Jimmy about how awesome he is, if we had a neighbor named Jimmy. I love this book and I hope all of you do as well. But I really like the fact that my dad isn't blabby about it and I really feel that you can't be that way with your kids if you want this to work. So, if you are a bragger, this isn't going to work for you. Your kid has to know that they can trust you.

I also think these letters are going to impact my future by showing me that I can do anything I put my mind to. No, I'm not saying this is all sugar plums and rainbows. And that makes another layer were corrections come in. (Read that chapter.) It is ok for us to be corrected, because it helps us to be put back on the right track. One example is when I was in sixth grade and my grades were plummeting seriously and I was making bad grades. I had also never had so many new friends. I really struggled. He wrote me in the letters and told me that "friends are important, but not as important as your grades." And you know, he was absolutely right. So, what I am saying is, these letters are eye opening because in the next letter, he says "Great job pulling up your grades." Overall, after all the things I have said, these letters mean the world to me and I would give anything for them.

Summary 2

On my perspective of getting letters every 14th of every month, I really enjoy it. I get them even if he misses the exact date. But I am ok as long as it isn't more than one day. But I just love them because my dad recognizes how hard I work on something. He always adds something I got better at. For example, I use to bite my nails and in one of the letters he told me how happy he was that I stopped biting them and he liked that I grew them out. I enjoy all of the great feedback me and my sisters get from him. It's like we get little pieces of him. One time he told me how happy he was of me for making AB honor roll and that made me so happy to hear. It was the first time I had ever really felt that way, because my grades were always my strug. It seems easier to make good grades, because I know in his letters, he is really pulling for me. I feel like if I didn't have the letters, I wouldn't feel sure about how he felt about how I am doing. Sometimes I will be really impatient in waiting for them and keep asking him what the date is. The letters really hit me in the feels sometimes, but they are like happy tears, because I know how he feels about me. I actually can't wait to get my next one, because I know he is going to talk about the concert we just had for band. I really appreciate the ones he writes about my birthdays too. I appreciate them so much; I can't say that enough. I love you dad and can't wait to get the next one.

Summary 3

For over a year now, patiently waiting to read the next letter sent from my dad each month has become a normal part of my life. The past six years, my dad and I have lived over 700 miles apart. It hasn't always been easy, but I can say the distance between us has only made us stronger. I remember being thirteen years old and him asking if I was fine with him moving away due to the great job opportunity he received. At first, I was honestly hesitant of what my answer would be but only because I was afraid of the enormous change it would put on my daily life with not being able to see him as much. As people, we always question if we will allow changes that are out of our comfort zone into our lives because we are unaware of what the outcome will be. I knew it was such a great opportunity for my dad, so I proceeded to encourage him to take the offer. To this day, I don't regret telling him to go at all because he has constantly made me feel just as important and loved as before. For example, the first couple of years he made a promise to come visit at least once a month and he did just that. Looking back on it now, I know that that was such a hard commitment due to the long distance between us, but my dad made me a top priority and kept his promise. I am forever grateful for the relationship me and my father have. When he first introduced the idea of writing letters to my siblings and I every month, it honestly surprised me because I had never heard of a father doing that for their children. Now, I couldn't imagine how it would be to not get them. It seems that every letter I receive from him comes right when I need them to. He decided that we should read the letters back to him and going over each letter with him is time that I will forever cherish. The letters encourage and inspire me to become a better version of myself. Getting feedback from my dad is honestly one of the best feelings. He notices and points out details maybe I wouldn't even think is important or even notice about myself. In every letter he has sent me, there has never been one negative statement and I believe that's important when writing the letters. My dad lets me know how happy he is with each and every one of my accomplishments and motivates me to work even harder. One thing I admire about my dad is when he truly dedicates himself, there's no stopping him. When he says he's going to do something you better believe it's done. When he decided to write this book, he set his mind to it and has continuously worked on it until it was done. One thing he is not is a procrastinator, he has never missed sending me a single letter. With my dad making the choice to write letters to my siblings and I has also benefited in the way I view my future self as a mother. I plan to do the same thing for my children when I'm older. I believe it's so important to obtain a great relationship between a child and a parent. My father has taught me that a parent's role is to nurture and obtain a healthy relationship with their children and to guide them in the right direction. One thing my dad has really helped me with is goal setting. Without goals what are you working towards? How do you achieve accomplishments without a plan to make it there? Goals are key for your future. With every goal I reach, I can't wait to share the news with my dad no matter how little or big it is. He has always pushed me to believe the sky's the limit and that anything can be done with hard work and dedication. My dad inspires me in so many ways and I couldn't be more thankful for the father that he is.

So, in summary, I hope what you've read has inspired you to put your best foot forward being a father. The foundation is there, the principles have been covered, and the points of reference are in your mind. Now it is up to you to apply what you have learned and make sure you put everything you can in balance and under the scrutiny of truth. Enjoy the journey!